To Auckland by the Ganges

To Auckland by the Ganges

The Journal of a Sea Voyage to New Zealand in 1863

edited and with an introduction by

Robert Grogans

Whittles Publishing

For my wife Julie, a wonderful and loving mother

Published by
Whittles Publishing Ltd.,
Dunbeath,
Caithness, KW6 6EG,
Scotland, UK

www.whittlespublishing.com

ISBN 978-184995-056-5

Printed by 4edge Limited, UK

Contents

Acknowledgements

The author gratefully thanks the Head of Rights and Information of Newsquest (Herald & Times) Ltd., for the kind permission to use the material that comprised the journal and which was published in thirteen instalments in the *Glasgow Herald* during January and February 1864.

Thanks are also due to the staff of the Mitchell Library, Glasgow for their assistance in providing facilities and requested materials.

A note on the editing

The journal by David Buchanan was written in a language and style that was standard for the time, particularly for publication in a newspaper such as the *Glasgow Herald*, which was produced for the discerning, educated and affluent readers who were mainly resident in mid-Victorian Clydeside.

To bring the journal before the modern reader, a degree of pruning and editing has been required. Many sentences were written in what is today a rather wordy and laboured style, with a tendency to add Latin words or phrases to the English text which were repetitive, superfluous and possibly confusing to many of us today. Punctuation such as the comma was liberally used, and the layout was structured, in the norm for the *Glasgow Herald* of the time, almost without paragraphs, which only appeared when a new day's narrative commenced.

Therefore to get an interesting work into a digestible format the journal has been edited taking the above points into account. The emphasis has been to preserve the flow and narrative of the original text, with endnotes used to explain references to people, events and places that may not be familiar to a 21st-century audience.

In addition, since the writer gave many accounts of the sails that were rigged at certain stages of the voyage, Appendix 1 describes a sailing ship's rigging. Appendix 2 provides a nautical glossary to the many nautical words and terms used. The remaining two appendices give a passenger list for the *Ganges* and a note about the ship.

Introduction

In 1863 there was only one method of mass movement of people from Britain to the other side of the world: by sailing ship, on a journey, depending upon the vagaries of wind and weather, that could take upwards of four months. A speedy passage in most cases would only be achieved by travelling non-stop, spurning the opportunity to break the tedium of the long voyage by calling at ports such as Rio de Janeiro in Brazil, or Cape Town in southern Africa.

Anyone who was prepared to take the time and risk the dangers of travel to such destinations invariably did so on government, professional or military service; or to seek out a better life through emigration, or a better climate for the good of their health. Until 1868 almost the only other group of people to travel such distances were convicts being transported. Tourists and leisurely travellers to the southern hemisphere were few and far between during the mid-19th century.

At that time in New Zealand the offer of grants of parcels of land was used by the British government and the colonial administration as a means of enticing emigrants to the fledgling colony, particularly if they possessed capital and a useful physical, mechanical or professional skill. One example was the eight hundred members of Nonconformist churches who emigrated to New Zealand, setting sail from London in June and July 1862, aboard four vessels, the *Matilda Wattenbach*, *William Miles*, *Ida Zeigler* and *Hanover*. Every emigrant who paid his or her passage was granted forty acres of land in a newly established area of the colony named Albertland.[1] There had been some scrutiny by the House of Commons in earlier years regarding an alleged scandal over the land grants scheme; it was, however, still in operation during the summer of 1863.

For one emigrant, a combination of health problems allied to a desire to seek better prospects for his family were the reasons for migrating to New Zealand. As an inducement he and his family had been allocated 120 acres of land, probably near to Auckland. Along with the wealthier passengers aboard the ship that took him and his family to New Zealand, the *Ganges*, he travelled cabin class, and dined at the captain's table.

The writer of the journal, David Buchanan, was born in Montrose, c.1807. This c.1891 view of the High Street would probably have changed little from his early childhood when he lived in the town. Courtesy of the University of St Andrews Library

In Scotland he had been a successful journalist, having been employed in an editorial role with an important Edinburgh-based newspaper, the *Caledonian Mercury*, until about 1859, before he moved to the west of Scotland, where he joined the staff of the prestigious, Tory-leaning *Glasgow Herald* in a similar capacity. His father had been involved with the *Caledonian Mercury* for a number of years at least until 1827, so that he had travelled along a reasonably well-smoothed career path.

His name was David Buchanan and he had been born in Montrose in north-east Scotland, a coastal town in the county of Angus, or Forfarshire as it is more commonly known. He moved as a young boy to Edinburgh, where his father appears to have established valued connections within the legal profession and among the city's political and professional elites, probably thanks to his journalistic activities which would have had distinct political overtones.

He was educated at the city's Royal High School[2], and given his family background, one would have expected him to have studied at university, but research has failed to find such evidence. He married Jessie Milne, in Gavrock, Kincardineshire on 24 June 1838. She was from successful farming people, and was eleven years his junior and a native of Kincardineshire, just south of Aberdeen. Jessie had died in Edinburgh in March 1855, during childbirth at the age of just 37, having borne her husband nine children, four of whom, three sons and one daughter, had died at a young age. A fifth died with her during that tragic birth.

Like another Edinburgher, the writer Robert Louis Stevenson, David was suffering from a debilitating illness and was advised by his doctors to move to a healthier climate. He chose New Zealand, and at the age of 55, along with his young son Robert, aged 11, and three daughters, Elizabeth, aged 23, Annabella, aged 18 and Sarah (more affectionately known as Sally), aged 14, sailed from Gravesend on the Thames at the close of June 1863.

Using his journalistic skills, Buchanan took the opportunity to maintain a daily journal of the voyage from the Thames to Auckland. His former connections with the newspaper allied to his literary skill ensured that the journal was serialised under the title *Life in an Emigrant Ship, by D. B.* over thirteen instalments. Published twice weekly in the *Glasgow Herald* several months after the end of the voyage, the narrative described the day-to-day activities of both passengers and crew.

He was adept at describing the changes in the arrangement and use of the ship's sails, and he did so with a knowledge of the handling of sailing ships through much personal sailing experience gained over many years in and around Scottish coastal waters. As the voyage on the *Ganges* progressed, he added a number of anecdotal tales and experiences he had encountered over the years, and gave some interesting snapshots of life in early to mid 19th-century Scottish society. For example, near the end of the journal he wrote an interesting piece that concerned the Earl of Dundonald in 1856, when the earl was in his eighties. The earl was, of course, none other than the 'Sea Wolf' himself, Admiral Thomas Cochrane, the Scot whom many considered an equal of Horatio Nelson among the giants of the celebrated Royal Navy commanders during the late 18th and early 19th centuries.

During his narrative Buchanan hints at his politics, which were certainly in tune with the *Glasgow Herald* of his time. His middle-class credentials were embodied by the fact that he lived among the wealthier residents of both Edinburgh and Glasgow, having resided at the then fashionable Edinburgh addresses of Raeburn Place and Broughton Street, and St George's Road in the west end of Glasgow. Domestic servants were employed by him to attend to his home and to his family's needs. Exemplifying much of the middle-class political opinion of the time, he saw little need for the extension of the franchise to greater swathes of the populace. Limited reform for the masses appeared to be his standpoint. Above all, he portrays himself as a typical middle-class inhabitant of Queen Victoria's Britain, in the middle years of her reign, with the prized beliefs that the monarchy, the established churches (although he makes no reference to the Catholic church or Catholic worship aboard ship), the rule of law, property ownership, the expanding British Empire, and the class system were all sacrosanct.

In the New Zealand spring of 1863, David Buchanan, his family and fellow emigrant passengers set foot upon a land that was subject to unrest, as the Maori wars were ongoing. As with the native Americans and in other British colonies such as South Africa and Australia, the encroachment of white settlers onto what was the land of the native New Zealanders had caused friction that ultimately led to violent confrontation. In mid-1863, during the winter months, Maori violence broke out in the Auckland area. A combination of businessmen and land speculators demanded military action, with the land of the rebel Maoris to be confiscated and offered to settlers. Around 400 single men who had settled in the town (later city) of Auckland, which had been established in 1840, were conscripted as a backup to the British regular troops and used in local defence duties. They were formed into a force known as the Forest Rangers.

During 1863 a worried British government sent 3,000 troop reinforcements from British bases in India, Ceylon and Burma (the latter two modern Sri Lanka and Myanmar respectively). By the middle of 1863 there were about 10,000 troops from 12 British imperial regiments based in New Zealand. What was an increasingly costly colonial war was generally fought out in the New Zealand bush country, mostly away from the larger centres of population. To the south of Auckland, where there were concentrations of Maoris who were anti-British and had refused an oath of allegiance to the British Crown, there were violent clashes between British and Maori armies in what became known as the Waikato and Tauranga campaigns. These were fought out during 1863–64, after which the British forces and the settlers along with those Maori peoples who had pledged allegiance to the Crown gradually gained full control of New Zealand in general and the area around Auckland in particular. A circumstance thrown up by these troubles was the discovery of gold in Auckland province. However, it was not until 1875 that prospectors were confident enough that the Maori problem had been resolved satisfactorily to start mining the gold. The Maori conflict was closely reported in British newspapers such as the *Glasgow Herald*, and it was not unusual to find lengthy reports of the Maori wars alongside news of that other tragic conflict, the American civil war, which had entered its closing stages at the time of the Buchanans' landing on New Zealand soil.

David Buchanan and his family may well have settled and led a prosperous life, but whatever the future held for him, one thing is certain: he is owed our gratitude for having written and left for posterity an interesting and valued account of experiences on a voyage in an age with a dominant mode of sea travel that has long since passed into history.

---

1. Albertland was located in the Northland administrative region to the north of Auckland, and is the northernmost area of the North Island of New Zealand.

2. The Royal High School was established in the 16th century. The school property in which Buchanan studied was demolished and replaced some years after his time there.

June 1863

23 June 1863 – It is one of the laws of nature which it requires no philosopher to discover – although Malthus[1] has beautifully elucidated it – that man must go in search of his food. We find the Esquimaux [Eskimos], as soon as their brief spring – or rather summer – commences, breaking up their snow hut encampments, and migrating to where they will find the chance of replenishing their exhausted stores, or procuring seals, or whatever the opening waters may throw in their way. The Red Indians of the Far West have, in like manner, to shift their wigwams and go in quest of other hunting grounds.

The same inexorable law also applies to civilised life. A farmer, for example, has four or five sons; one may stay at home to aid, and in the course of time succeed his father; the others may go forth into the busy cities to push their way, or, perhaps, across the waters to our distant colonies, there to pursue their industry, and be incorporated into young and rapidly rising communities.

Such were my thoughts today, as Gravesend bells chimed 12 o'clock noon, and I found myself with my family, standing on the quarter deck of the *Ganges* (of Willis, Gann & Co.'s line), which was appointed to sail that afternoon for Auckland, New Zealand. All was, of course, confusion on the decks.

The great body of the steerage or emigrant passengers[2] had joined the ship three days before in the London docks, and were busily intent on the serving out of their rations at the cook's galley. Others were, however, arriving with their bedding and other belongings slung over their shoulders.

Then there was such a medley of sounds – the squeaking of the pigs, the cackling of geese, the 'quack-quack' of the ducks, and the crowing of the cocks in the coops, not to speak of the squalls among the children – that one might have imagined having been planted in the centre of a farm-yard instead of aboard ship.

The Government officials came on board at three o'clock, and the inspection of the passengers commenced, as also of the ship and stores. Dinner was served up in the cabin, but there were the friends of passengers aboard and partaking of the hospitalities of the *Ganges*, so that we could not tell who were to be our fellow-passengers on a far-distant voyage.

At six o'clock in the evening, however, the order was given for all to go ashore who were not accompanying the ship; then there were those sad farewells – which were accompanied with the waving of handkerchiefs between those in the boats, as they left the ship's side, and those who remained on board – longing eyes being strained on either side to catch the last glimpse of those whom they might never meet again in this world. Such scenes, of course, are of every day occurrence, but they are not the less painful to those whom they concern.

The cheering chant of the sailors was soon heard as they commenced to weigh, and at seven o'clock the anchor came home and the *Ganges* swung rapidly round with the stream. We proceeded down to the Nore[3] in tow of two tugs, and there anchored for the night. Some of the emigrants struck up *Home, sweet home*, which others did not deem an appropriate ditty, and were more inclined for *Cheer, boys cheer*.

We retired to our berths which we found wonderfully comfortable, and slept soundly after all the business and anxieties of the day. Indeed, I dare say the feeling of nearly one and all was that of thankfulness that they were finally afloat – so great had been the toil and hurry of the preceding few weeks, in carrying out the necessary preparations.

24 June – A beautiful morning. We again weighed anchor, and were taken in tow by our two tugs. At eight we found ourselves off Margate, and all was looking serene on both sea and shore. When off the Tongue floating-light,[4] the order was given to run up the jibs, tighten the starboard braces, and slacken the weather-port braces. The object of the last manoeuvre was, of course, to lay the yards in the direction of the wind. All these operations were interesting in the eyes of a landsman.

Immediately afterwards the mizzen gaff or spanker was hoisted, then down came skysails, royals, topgallant and topsails[5] – in time, the vessel was nearly covered with canvas. At half-past nine we parted with the tugs, and our ship was left to its own resources, as we rounded the North Foreland, and entered the Downs. There was scarcely a breath of wind, but as our Channel pilot said to our captain, 'We might be thankful that we had any at all.' As it was, we made way by the aid of our top or smaller sails, which were comparatively easily filled.

A Deal boat boarded us, and the boatman demanded the modest recompense of 1s for every letter he carried ashore[6]. The passengers fore and aft amused themselves as best they could. There were chess and cards on the poop deck, and all manner of light literature. In the forward area of the ship the young men engaged in leaping and other athletic exercises. At three o'clock, however, as we were off the heights of Dover, the wind freshened, and the *Ganges* commenced to sail in earnest. There was no doubt of her sailing capabilities.

I may mention that our vessel was built at Boston in 1855, and is rated at 1,200 old tons register, and 3,000 tons burthen. Our commander, Captain Thomas Funnell,[7] was a fine specimen of a British seaman, and this was his first voyage in the *Ganges*, but he has had experience in the Indian and Australian trade.

We made a fine run in the afternoon, and expected to be off the Isle of Wight at six o'clock on the following morning, where we were to land our Channel pilot, who was to carry ashore what would probably be our final communications. The sky, however, looked suspicious at nine o'clock in the evening.

We were also beginning to experience the value of water. Yesterday we were indifferent about the matter, for in the bustle aboard ship we probably did not get our full quantum, and we found ourselves without a drop on going to bed, the supply having been stopped for the day. However, I managed, as a favour, to procure less than half a pint from the steward for my little boy. The lesson has taught us to husband our supply, for it is amply sufficient for all our purposes if we keep in mind the wholesome adage – *Waste not, want not.*

25 June – Our anticipations as to the signs of the weather last night were proven correct. Then, at about eleven o'clock p.m., the rain had came down and thunder and lightning succeeded. The flashes were very vivid, and lit up the waters, vessels being distinctly visible at a considerable distance. There was a great hurrying to and fro on deck. Sail was taken in as fast as possible, and as the pilot said, 'Not too soon.'

Instead of nearing the Isle of Wight we were carried a long way in the direction of the French coast. I looked out on the quarter deck about three o'clock a.m., when the wind had somewhat abated, though the ship was rolling heavily. The scene was very animated, and there was much to do as the nautical evolutions succeeded each other rapidly. The chant of our sailors ran something like this – 'The ship's a-rolling, a-rolling, going, going, go-o-o,' and then came the long and the strong pull. Towards seven o'clock in the morning the weather had moderated, and none in the cabin seemed greatly the worse for the ship's rolling during the night.

At 12 noon our course was changed from south-west to north-east, or in the direction of the Isle of Wight, which we descried directly in the distance at about four o'clock, when we signalled a pilot smack, in which our pilot went ashore with a box of letters. Probably the last opportunity that we would have of communicating with the land. Several of our lady passengers and also a few of our gentlemen, showed signs of distress.[8] Although we had, as usual, an excellent and varied table, there were a good few vacancies at dinner.

The wind continued adverse, though the weather was very quiet. There was, therefore, nothing for it but to beat to and fro. On our south by south-west tack at 11 o'clock at night we came within sight of the light at Barfleur, on the coast of France, where the battle of La Hogue commenced in 1692;[9] then we fetched across on the opposite tack to the Isle of Wight, and so on.

26 June – At eight in the morning we were again in sight of the coast of France, about Flamanville, in Normandy. The day was fine, but that south-west or head wind still continued, and the evening found us back on the English coast, with that weary Isle of Wight still visible to the eastward. I do not think we had made 30 miles within the last 24 hours. How we longed for a stiff north-easter!

The emigrants were very jolly. Leap-frog was going on, and also some game introduced by our passengers from Pollokshaws,[10] in which one stood with his eyes shut and his hands clasped on his ears. Players behind gave a sharp slap on one of the hands of the player thus standing, whose cue was to turn quickly round and detect the slapper, seizing him by one of the ears. The person thus comprehended, had then to take the place of his captor.

The emigrants' captains of the messes could be seen, each bearing a coarse linen bag down their hatchway, which was labelled with a steel ticket, indicating the number of their respective messes. It contained their supply of pudding which was in their rations for the day.

The cabin passengers were getting more familiar with each other. There are some fine young gentlemanly Englishmen among them, and we have a few ladies. The former baited their fishing hooks today and threw their lines over the stern, but no result, though we anticipated better success when we got into other latitudes.

Later it began to rain slightly, and there was the prospect of a rather dirty night, but our comfort was that it promised signs of a change of wind. So we would go to rest easier.

Solaced by that hope, I was marked down for a match at chess one of these days. It is a long time since I studied Philidor,[11] the great chess authority of former days; but I must do my best to sharpen up my game before I encounter my challenger, a newly met Gloucestershire friend.

27 June – This is the fourth day that we have been beating up the Channel, and we have been etching very little way, as the wind still continued ahead. The night was thick – and the wind rose, and the vessel rolled.

My little fellow got up as usual and dressed, but was soon glad to again seek the shelter of his berth. There had been a great deal of sickness during the night, and a considerable mess of it between decks.

No ladies appeared in the cabin at breakfast, and there were also several absentees among the male passengers. It was a pity, for they lost a most substantial meal. We had beef steaks, mutton chops, cold meat, potatoes, and hot rolls; for we have our baker as well as butcher on board.

During breakfast our Captain gave me a most interesting detail of the burning of the *Eastern City*,[12] a Glasgow ship, off the South America coast, in 1858. He was the first officer of the transport vessel,[13] with troops on board, which came to the rescue, and had to take charge of the first boat that proceeded to the *Eastern City*.

He managed to get on board with great difficulty, owing to the heavy sea running at the time; and the scene he then witnessed beggared description. Many of the crew were in a state of intoxication, for they had mutinied and forced open the spirit stores.

By great efforts, and by swinging those on board the burning vessel from the cross-jack into the boats of the transport, and the long-boat of the *Eastern City*, which was the only one of the latter ship available, they providentially succeeded in rescuing all on board – some 250 – without a single scratch. The rescued crew proved very troublesome customers when taken on board the transport, but the troops soon managed to bring them under subjection.

We had a bit of a swell today, and continued beating to and fro but the stewards have fenced the tables. There were numerous applications for brandy from the forward passengers, but that could only be given to them as a medical remedy, and by the authority of the doctor. I can, however, see that it is a very popular medicine, and deemed a panacea for all complaints. One sturdy old Yorkshire ploughman I saw come aft, saying he wanted a *soep* of brandy for his sick folks. If he was successful in his mission, I suspect the brandy would have paid a toll in its transit to the patients.

This day only seven of us, inclusive of the captain and the doctor, mustered at dinner, and no ladies; but the swell abated towards evening. Sea legs were in requisition.

I may mention that we have about 260 souls aboard, inclusive of 41 attached to the ship – viz., captain and three officers, surgeon, purser, carpenter, boatswain, sailmaker, baker, butcher, 18 able bodied seamen, four ordinary seamen and the remainder of the 41 comprising apprentices, stewards, and cooks, three of the stewards being attached to the cuddy, which provided us with excellent attention.

28 June – This was the first Sunday of our voyage. The morning was lovely; a gentle breeze, with a slight tremor on the waters. There was a delightful feeling in the atmosphere, so mild and pure, and such as one rarely experienced in Scotland, even at your favourite watering places on the estuary of the Clyde.

Last night, on our south tack, we came nigh to the Island of Alderney; then across on the opposite tack, to the Devonshire coast. The wind was a point or two less unfavourable, but there was so little of it that our log only gave us four knots in the hour.

At ten o'clock a.m., ladders were placed across the quarter deck, with planks on the steps for seats, and the Rev. Mr. Anderson, late of the Original Secession Church, Kilwinning,[14] took his place behind the after companion to perform public worship. In the evening the Church of England service was read to the cabin passengers on the poop deck by a young Irish gentleman, of Trinity College, Dublin, and who intended to take holy orders in New Zealand. He had been a few years in China. There is another Scotch clergyman on board – the Rev. Mr. Smith, late of Pollokshaws. Those in the forward part of the ship will, therefore, be at no loss for pastoral superintendence on board the *Ganges*.

The evening found us still knocking to and fro in the Channel under a fresh but adverse wind. We were off Portland, and last night we were nearly in the same position, so that we are doing little more than holding our own.

29 June – 'Ech! Anither bra' day!' as the Highlandman, accustomed to his own drizzly, uncertain clime, said after he had been four or five days within the tropics, and saw the sun rise each successive morning with renewed splendour.[15] No improvement in the wind, but the weather is so fine that the passengers appeared indifferent as to the progress.

The ladies are assembled aft of the poop, a space somewhat analogous to the stern gallery of a ship of war, only that it is above the main deck. Here they are seated on cushions reading and sewing. The gentlemen are reclined around them, and all was going merrily which set the tone for the day.

Towards afternoon we approached near to the Start-Point Lighthouse,[16] and had a distinct view of the cliffs of Devonshire. In the evening, after another tack, we returned to the English coast, and found the Start-Point still in view.

30 June – We had been a week afloat since leaving Gravesend, and working our way against westerly winds. This morning we had tacked across in the direction of Ushant Isle, off the coast of Bretagne, but we did not expect to get another glimpse of the land.

Today was the warmest day we have had, bright sunshine, and the air delightfully pure. There was scarcely a breath of wind, and the sails were flapping lazily against the masts. We were not making one knot in the hour.

All were, however, in good spirits, and various amusements were going on, both fore and aft. Towards evening a breeze sprang up, which was in our favour, but not of any great strength.

---

1. A reference to the Reverend T. R. Malthus, 1766–1834, an economist and clergyman, who believed that mankind could not continue to feed a rapidly expanding world population, and that birth control would be a requirement to overcome the problem.

2. An early reference to the economic distinction between steerage class and cabin class passengers. Those in steerage class were quartered in more densely populated and generally less salubrious accommodation.

3. Near the edge of the Thames estuary.

4. Located a few miles north of Margate, alerting shipping of sandbanks as the Thames opens out into the North Sea.

5. For description of sails see Appendix 1.

6. The equivalent of £3.64 at 2009 values using the Retail Price Index (R.P.I.). *www.measuringworth.com*

7. Although Buchanan names the ship's captain as Thomas Funnell, some official records name him as Theodore Funnell.

8. A reference to seasickness.

9. The sea battles of Barfleur and La Hogue, near Cherbourg on the Cotentin peninsula of Normandy, France, took place between 29 May and 4 June 1692. The result was a victory for English naval forces over those of the French, who were attempting to organise a fleet of ships to carry troops to invade England and reinstall James II to the throne and overthrow King William of Orange.

10. At the time of this journal Pollokshaws was a small but growing village to the south of Glasgow. It was annexed by Glasgow City Council in the late 19th century.

11. François André Danican Philidor was an 18th-century French composer of operas, and a chess master. Although he composed 21 operas he gained greater financial rewards through his chess acumen. He published a book in

1749 titled *Analysis of the Game of Chess*. It is recorded that he once beat two opponents simultaneously while blindfolded.

12. The *Eastern City* sailed from Liverpool on 10 July 1858 with 184 emigrant passengers bound for Australia. On 23 August the vessel caught fire and a day later most of the passengers and crew were rescued by a British troopship and a merchant vessel, the *Marco Polo*, and taken to Cape Town. The *Eastern City* sank after the rescue, on 24 August 1858.

13. The transport vessel was the *Merchantman*, which had been bound for Calcutta.

14. Kilwinning is a small town in the west of Scotland, located in the north-west part of the county of Ayrshire.

15. A reference to 'another fine day' often encountered by the many Scottish Highland infantrymen posted to warmer climes while serving with the British Highland army regiments.

16. Situated at Start Bay to the south of Torquay on the edge of the south Devon coastline.

July 1863

1 July – On awakening, we soon discovered by the pitching of the ship and the noise outside that the wind had freshened and was blowing stiffly. It came from the south, and enabled us to steer west by north-west, which was comparatively favourable, although south-west was our regular course.

We had now reached the mouth of the [English] Channel, and were making in the direction of the Scilly Islands. The ship was driving through the waves at the rate of eight knots, and we certainly felt the intentions of the Atlantic.

Many passengers were confined to their berths; still the day was pleasant enough to those who were well. For my own part, I greatly preferred those long flowing billows to the nasty short, chopping sea, which a south-wester causes off the coast of Arran in Scotland.[1] Although I saw our bows mounting and falling, I experienced no difficulty in writing these little details.

At eight o'clock in the evening the wind had started to rise, and we were driving southward as if bound for the coast of Ireland, instead of the Bay of Biscay. The ship was lurching and the weather threatening.

2 July – We have had a stormy night, with the ship rolling and dancing to and fro. She would not stay on course, so that our commander had no resource but to travel west, or put her on to the wind, by which we lost our intended direction.

I thought I had got all secure in my cabin, but I found that, do what may, something got loose and went on the run. My little fellow[2] had left some small wooden bowl on a shelf, which commenced to roll back and fore with every pitch of the vessel and, as I learned in the morning, had been too well heard by the inmates of the cabins on either side. My boy and I fortunately slept well, which few did that night. Between decks basins, cans, and other utensils got loose; there was a regular rumpus throughout the night.

In the forenoon the wind fell, but there was a good deal of swell – the ship only made about three knots. Towards evening there came a fine breeze, and we were going through the Bay of Biscay[3] about south-west, or nearly in the desired direction, at seven or eight knots. During the morning a homeward bound vessel signalled us for the longitude, which was given at 8° 27' W.

3 July – A quiet delightful morning. We felt aware of the change of climate as we headed south. The wind was from north-east, and we were steering south-west, which is exactly what our direction ought to be; but unfortunately, we have had very little wind. The Bay of Biscay was as smooth as the Clyde channel off Dumbarton Castle,[4] and there was an undulation, and a constant unsteady motion.

If those leaving the Broomielaw on this (Friday) afternoon for Millport, Rothesay, Dunoon,[5] and the other snug retreats on the beautiful Firth of Clyde, were to find their steamer suddenly floating where we were now, there would be a bit of a sensation aboard; many would exclaim, 'What can the matter be!' as they heard the doors of the cabins go 'bang, bang' on their hinges.

Later, we raised the studding sails on the main and fore masts and made some headway through the smooth water, and at about 8 p.m. the breeze freshened, and we sailed along at seven knots.

4 July – There was a fine fair wind this morning, and we ran before it comfortably at 10 knots. There was nothing to be seen except a brig far to the north-westward.

A few incidents have been occurring on board. Yesterday I saw the surgeon extract a tooth from a little chap; he had also to dress a cut which one of our sailors received on the hand; but I am happy to say that on the whole, his duties have been very light as yet.

The day continued fine, and how genial the climate had become. At 12 o'clock observations were taken, and gave latitude 44° 8' N., longitude 11° 27' W., which I found to be about 70 miles north-west of Cape Ortegal, on the coast of Spain.

The breeze stiffened as the day advanced; we were going beautifully with a pile of canvas spread out, including skysails, spanker, trysail, and studding sails. This was by far the most satisfactory day we have had. A continuance of such weather would, in a few days, bring us within the tropics.

Earlier today we had a raid into the hold, and I got hold of my books, which was a great comfort. These included some of Cooper's[6] tales of the sea, which I have always preferred, even to those of Captain Marryat,[7] admirable as *Midshipman Easy* is. The Long Tom Coffin of Cooper is one of those original characters and creations of genius that may stand comparison with those of Sir Walter Scott; and of all the contemporaries of the latter, none came so near to him as his American rival. The two once met each other in Paris, where they were for the time the lions of the literary world.

'A wee before the sun gaed doun'[8] – which it did in our present latitude about three-quarters of an hour or an hour (allowing for the difference in time) before it would cease to shine on the Cathedral of Glasgow – I found myself engaged with two young Englishmen on that classic pastime, pitch and toss. The main tactic was to watch the motion of the ship, and, at the nick of time, let fly the halfpenny at the goal. I succeeded pretty well, for I found myself at the close of the revels plus a few coppers.

In the evening the breeze kept up; the moon and stars shone out, Venus being the first to come forth; and how beautiful it was to look over the waters of the dark blue sea.

5 July – This was our second Sunday at sea, and the weather was all that we could desire. A fine breeze carried us along at about eight knots, under a cloud of sail.

The Presbyterian service took place in forenoon and afternoon, as on the former Sunday; while the Church of England service was conducted in the saloon, by our friend of Trinity College,[9] in the morning and evening. One of our young men led the musical part of the English service on a small harmonium, and the choir, in the circumstances, was very efficient.

At 12 p.m. we stood in latitude 41° 26' N., longitude 12° 59'W., or about 280 miles off the mouth of the Douro. A shoal of porpoise came nigh to us in the afternoon, and, for a time, rather discomposed those engaged in the afternoon Presbyterian service, who were assembled on the quarter deck. How smart some of our Jack-a-tars looked today in their Sunday togs.

The evening was lovely, Venus (or our evening star) again shone forth with her satellite in dazzling brightness; and in a while Ursa Major appeared, and the heavens unfolded their splendour. The night breeze freshened, and our speed increased.

She travels! She travels!

6 July – Another beautiful day; calm, and scarcely a breath of wind stirred, so that our vast expanse of canvas carried the *Ganges* onward only at about two knots.

We felt the heat today, although not unpleasantly. We were, however, donning lighter raiment. Some passengers were studying Greek and mathematics; others were engaged in cutting down their tobacco; one or two amused themselves firing at a bottle swung over the taffrail, and attached by a line. Several bottles have already been shattered after that fashion. The ladies were plying all manner of plain and fancy work.[10] For myself, I had to play the schoolmaster to my boy.

At 12 o'clock noon today, we were in latitude 39° 23' N., longitude 13° 26' W. The sun went down at 7.25 p.m. by our time. In contrast, it set in your quarter at 8.57 p.m. The Atlantic remained as calm as a mill pond, but our skysails and royals on the mainmast were drawing a little.

7 July – The day was fine and the heat nicely tempered by a light breeze, which carried us along about 5½ knots. We had an awning spread over the poop, and a balmy atmosphere underneath.

Among 260 human beings, exposed to the vicissitudes of a long voyage, mischances will occur. Yesterday afternoon a fine young man, one of the cabin stewards, swallowed by mistake some disinfecting fluid (chloride of lime and corrosive sublimate). The surgeon was in instant attendance, and administered the proper antidote. Had the relief been postponed or not available, death would have ensued within a brief period.

Today the patient is of course poorly, but no worse than anticipated. In the forenoon a child fell down the midships hatchway and dislocated a collar bone.

At 12 o'clock noon today we were in latitude 38° 6' N., longitude 14° 55' W. The wind continued fair but light, so that we had not averaged above five knots throughout the day. At night a swell arose, indicating that it had been blowing hard in some quarter of the Atlantic. The ship rolled, and I suspected that it would be a restless night with quite a few.

8 July – In the morning the sun shone forth, and there was fortunately a stiff breeze. There had been a good deal of sickness between decks, and no little noise during the night, in consequence of some of the casks in the stores having got loose. Happily, for myself, I had learned all that in the morning, as I am not easily disturbed when tiredness overcomes the noise. The steward who swallowed the poisonous fluid is doing well, and will resume his duty in a day or two.

At 12 o'clock noon today our position was latitude 36° 29' N., longitude 16° 30' W., or about 208 miles north and 57 miles east of Madeira.

9 July – Another beautiful day, but the sun was powerful enough to make one court the shade. A slight breeze carried us onward under a cloud of sail, at about six knots.

Several of Mother Cary's chickens[11] have greeted us, which are the only objects we have seen on the wide waste of waters, as we have not descried a sail for the last three days.

At 12 noon we were in latitude 34° 28' N., longitude 18° 18' W. We had hoped to obtain a distant glimpse of Madeira before nightfall, but we were too far to the westward.

As night fell the evening star shone out as usual, and the firmament was soon afterwards ablaze with stars. At eight o'clock we were making seven knots, and at 10 p.m. we had increased to eight knots. The dew was falling heavily, and soft music floated along the deck from the harmonium, accompanied by several voices.

10 July – The wind continued fair, and we got along nicely on our south-west by west course. What a succession of lovely days we have had; but as we are expected to be within the tropics in a few days, we may well feel the heat rather oppressive.

We have reached latitude 31° 58' N., longitude 19° 30' W., or some way to the north of the Canary Islands, and we are sailing steadily at seven knots. A turtle was seen close to the ship, but there was no chance of capturing it unless a boat could have been lowered. Our captain on one occasion caught 21 off the Western Isles.[12]

Buchanan was educated at the old Royal High School in the city of Edinburgh during the early part of the 19th century. This sketch of the building in which he was taught the curriculum was demolished in the later years to be replaced by a new building which has survived to the present day, and which was used for a few years for the Scottish Parliament – from 1999 until the opening of the current seat of Scottish Government. One of Buchanan's student predecessors was Sir Walter Scott, who was educated in the same premises in which Buchanan studied. Reproduced with acknowledgement to Peter Stubbs www.edinphoto.org.uk

11 July – A fine fair wind, smooth sea, and all sail set. By way of diversifying the recreations, one of our intermediate passengers produced boxing gloves, and we had one or two spirited little contests.

Two tall men went at it and pounded away with more good will than science. Two little Englishmen then went on, who were more expert in the art.

The onlookers clustered so eagerly around that I had to mount into the rigging to obtain a proper view of the edifying spectacle. One of the combatants was a thick-set little figure, and had the better ballast of the two, but the other was the more nimble, and made one or two very pretty hits, which were, however, duly requited. One evolution where the lighter man hit, then ducked, and suddenly whirled round to elude the counter of his antagonist, drew down loud applause.

Although we were in the latitude of the Canary Islands and the Sahara Desert of Africa, there was a cool breeze, which rendered the temperature very pleasant. Later, as we were reminded by one of our officers, this was Saturday night at sea, and a little extra festivity was legitimate. A refreshment was served in the saloon and the standing toast was, 'The wind that blows, and the ship that goes, and the lass that loves the sailor.'

Latitude 29° 32' N., longitude 20° 41' W.

12 July – Today was our third Sunday at sea. The temperature was warm, but we have had a nice breeze which carried us along. The Church of England service was performed in the saloon in the morning and in the evening, and the Presbyterian service as usual.

Latitude 26° 56' N., longitude 21° 54' W.

13 July – It was decidedly hot today, but it is nothing to what we may yet expect. The thermometer stood at 74F in the shade. Several flocks of flying fish have appeared, but we have not seen a sail for a week. Some of us would dearly like a swim; as it is we must be contented with a bucket of salt water and the application of the sponge.

We have had a fine breeze, and have made good progress, and sailed along at from seven to eight knots. The captain called my attention to my shadow, and when I looked down on the deck I found it was scarcely a foot long, so that the sun must have been rather vertical or overhead. Towards the night the wind freshened, and the *Ganges'* sails began to pay out.

It had became dark earlier, for at seven o'clock in the evening we could not see to read with daylight. The dew was also falling heavily on our decks, so that at a comparatively early hour this evening there was a strong muster in the saloon. Whist and cribbage, reading and conversation, passed away the night.

Latitude 24° 29' N., longitude 22° 30' W.

14 July – We have had a fine wind throughout the night, which has brought us within the tropics, and this morning it fortunately continued. The vessel was going at from nine to ten knots, and rolled a little, as the waves showed their white crests, but on the whole her motion was wonderfully steady. The flying fish were seen disporting around.

While I was writing (at 10 a.m.) a sail was sighted ahead, and evidently a considerable vessel, going in the same course as ourselves. The *Ganges* was making up with her, so that there was a chance of having a talk, which would be rather an interesting event to us all. Our Pollokshaws and Barrhead[13] friends, of whom there were a considerable number forward, no doubt hoped it may prove a Clyde ship.

By 2 p.m. we had come up with the stranger, and our signal halyards were at work. The number of the *Ganges*, 4182, under her first distinguishing pendant, was signalled, and the number of the other vessel given in return.

She proved to be the barque *Cosmopolite*, of and from London, for Buenos Aires, and out 26 days. We have been out only 19, reckoning from the time our pilot was discharged, so that we have gained seven days on this vessel. We soon passed her, and in an hour or two she was far on our lee.

When we parted with the *Cosmopolite*, which we did, by dipping the British ensign three times – a nautical courtesy borrowed from the Dutch – a solitary swallow was seen following in our wake for about fifty miles, when, exhausted, the bird came to us, and was rescued. It remained all night, and was fed and delicately tended. In the morning it would be sent out, and hopefully it would return to the safety of landward.

Towards evening the sea was rising, but we were going bravely along with our studding sails still set. And what a racket the children were making forward as the ship rolled. There may be some sea sickness tonight, but not much, as our passengers have been getting more used to the vicissitudes of ocean life.

Our latitude today was 22° 6' N., longitude 24° 23' W., or about 400 to 600 miles off Cape Blanco on the African coast, and 300 miles north of St. Antonio, the northmost of the Cape de Verd Islands.

15 July – How the vessel rolled this morning, as she had been doing throughout the night. Few have complained of sickness, but there was many a complaint about the lack of sleep. I am thankful to have been in the condition of fine slumber, for I have no story to tell in connection with the events of the night, except that one of the stun-sail halyards gave way, which was a very trifling mishap.

As for myself and my little fellow, when we rose in the morning, I should quote Dryden1[14]: 'Here we stand, Woundless and well; may Heaven's high name be blessed for't.'

Our speed has been great in fact, when I looked over the taffrail this morning, the *Ganges* seemed to be travelling like a race-horse, as the foam seethed round her bows.

We have reached latitude 18° 42' N., longitude 23° 10' W., or about 90 miles off St. Antonio. That necessitated a change in our course to several points further westward, in order to give the island a good offing, for I find that sailors are no way partial to land. The swallow rescued the previous day had forsaken us, having probably scented St. Antonio Island.

Some of us were often anxious to know how far off we bear from the nearest land, but our captain and officers gave little heed to those inquiries. With them it is enough to feel that they have ample sea room. The aversion of Tom Coffin[15] to land was no great deviation from that entertained by seamen on the long voyage, however quaintly it may have been expressed.

That old salt remarked, 'Give me plenty of sea room, and good canvas, where there is no occasion for pilots at all. For my part, I was born on board a Chebaccoman,[16] and never could see the case of more land than now and then a small island, to raise a few vegetables, and to dry your fish. I'm sure the sight of it always makes me uncomfortable, unless we have the wind dead off shore.'

16 July – The wind has fallen, and with it the sea, leaving nothing save a slight swell on the smooth water. Several dolphins have appeared, as also has the nautilus, or Portuguese man-of-war, a bright little fish. One dolphin was hooked, but unfortunately the line broke before it could be got over the bulwark.

It was precious hot today, and it induced the wearing of very slight attire. Despite the heat there is nothing like keeping busy, for though any physical effort may be uncomfortable, it does help to avoid the possibility of boredom.

Towards the afternoon three dolphins were caught, and also some bonito. Several sail were in sight in the distance; one ahead in our course, which we will probably have passed during the night.

As the sun was going down there was sparring forward. The ship's baker, a thin sallow looking man, who once lived within the sound of London's Bow Bells, put on the gloves, and had a set-to with the sailmaker, who was rather proficient in the art. The latter however, had no chance with our 'master of the rolls', who gave the sailmaker one punch in the ribs with his left hand which, for a moment, took the wind from him.

Our butcher also entered the arena, and showed himself evidently no novice in the science. So far as I could learn, I do not think any of our Barrhead or Pollokshaws neighbours were ambitious to shine in that line.

Today we were in latitude 16° 24'N., longitude 25° 59' W., so we were gradually nearing the line [equator], and may cross it before the close of next week, if the wind would serve us, but we fear that we may be more or less becalmed. The thermometer today stood at 79F in the shade.

17 July – Very hot this day and calm. We have changed our course more to southward by south-east, but have made little progress. It was still satisfactory to find that we had made up on the vessel which we saw ahead of us yesterday, and passed it at four o'clock this morning.

That vessel, so far as could be judged when daylight showed her, did not seem to be obeying her helm very steadily in the calm weather.

Several of us have dispensed with coats and braces, and confined ourselves to woollen shirts, to find that at noon we were in latitude 15° 47' N., longitude 26° 35'W., with a temperature of 88F in the shade. In the evening the sun went down at 6.10 p.m.

18 July – 'Another broiler,' as old Cobbett[17] said when he was keeping the diary of his residence on his farm in Long Island; but we must make the best of it. Some of our young men have slept on deck and got the benefit of a bucket or two of salt water in the morning before coming down to their toilet.

Several pilot fish had been seen off our stern, which were generally the heralds of a shark. What rare sport it would be if we could hook one of those monsters of the deep. I trust we shall have such an adventure before we are done with our cruise. The ship was going slowly to the southward, and at that rate it will be a good while before we reach the line.

One of our passengers pulled out a *Scotsman*[18] newspaper today, dated 25th May last. It caused a momentary sensation, as if it had been the morning paper of the day. It is now nearly a month since we have had any tidings of what is doing on *terra firma*. General Lee[19] may have fought a great battle in Maryland or Virginia, and the Poles may have made head against the Czar of Russia, for all that we know.

At all events, this was the day on which the Court of Session rises – and that used to be the precursor of a blythe night in days of yore, when Jeffrey, Moncreiff, Cockburn, John Hope, Rutherford, and the glorious Patrick Robertson were in their zenith. Jeffrey would have been dispensing his elegant hospitalities at Tusculum (Craigcrook) and Harry Cockburn would have been off to his lovely Bonaly in the Pentland hills.[20]

We have gained little way during the last 24 hours, as we were only in latitude 15° 27' N., longitude 25° 55' W., so that the ship had been easting. The temperature was 83F in the shade, but I still did not feel the heat so oppressive on the whole; one would almost bear it for the sake of the luxury it imparts to a bath.

Three vessels were in sight, one astern and two on the port bow. Our position today would be about 100 miles off the St. Jago Islands.[21] A slight shower had fallen and the breeze was freshening.

19 July – Last night at about 11 o'clock, a large vessel approached us, and we expected that she would have hailed us, as she was to the windward, and therefore in that most favourable position for speaking; but she made no sign as she crossed our bows, her course being two points to the westward of us. Over the day several vessels had been in sight, and which we had passed during the night.

Divine service took place as usual. During the Presbyterian worship I saw from the poop several in the back row listening attentively to the service, and at the same time quietly smoking their pipes. While on a long sea voyage that did not seem to be considered discourteous.

I saw a bonito today, leaping and plunging in pursuit of a flying fish. It was a most animated chase, and so near that I could distinctly see both pursuer and pursued as they emerged in the air. Before sunset several barracouta appeared, careering close to us. Several lines were thrown overboard to get a chance of catching those large fish, but without success.

The temperature today was 82F in the shade, but we fortunately had a nice breeze which had carried us along. We have gained latitude 14° 42' N., longitude 25° 27' W.

20 July – It had been very warm and close throughout the night, but a breeze took us along at about five knots and during the morning we had a heavy but brief shower.

Four vessels were in sight ahead of us. One of them is so near that we can descry the awning on her decks, which showed that she must be a passenger ship.

By 11 o'clock a.m. it was discovered that it was a Spanish vessel (the *Conception*) of about 800 tons, bound for Manila, and 11 days out from the Isle of Mackinaw, as indicated by the signal-book and the chronicle of shipping; but the said Island of Mackinaw we have not succeeded in finding on the charts. It is one of the St. Antonio group,[22] but must be an insignificant spot of earth on the great surface of the globe.

The wind had died away, and we were not making above half a knot. Latitude 12° 49'N., longitude 23° 2' W. Temperature 82F in the shade.

21 July – We have been a month at sea today, and thus far we had got on excellently well. The cabin passengers are happily well associated, and there are one or two very intelligent and agreeable ladies and gentlemen in the intermediate department.

Last night we were all assembled aft the poop in the stern galley. The moon shone forth brightly on the waters, the air was soft and balmy, as if tempered by the ocean after being wafted from the great desert of Africa; in short, the scene was lovely, and it was enhanced by song – for there were a few good voices among our company.

In the morning the thermometer stood at 81F, but it would rise as the day advanced. We had made little headway, and had upwards of 800 miles between us and the Equator. In other words, we were about half-way through the tropic of Cancer.

The ships which we saw yesterday were still near to us, amidst the calm weather. The *Ganges* has as yet shown her heels to every vessel we have met on the same course; but our Spanish friend – the *Conception* – which was still pretty close on our port quarter, seemed a craft likely to test our mettle when the wind freshened.

At one o'clock p.m. a breeze had come, and up went our spanker. The Spaniard has also spread out his duck, and showed his stunsail royals. For a time the two vessels seemed to be pretty fairly matched, but before long it was evident that the Spaniard was gaining upon us, and at nightfall he was considerably ahead.

If there had been a stronger wind the result would probably have been different.

Latitude 11° 35' N., longitude 24° 33' W. Temperature 82F.

22 July – Last night we had a copious shower, which lasted nearly an hour, and cooled the decks. Water was a very different element, in our estimation, from what it was a month ago; accordingly, all sorts of utensils were in requisition to catch the rain as it flowed off the poop. Some of our Scotch passengers were especially zealous in their efforts, and exhibited their national thrift.

It was very warm today, and with scarcely a breath of wind; but several of us had set about our tasks, as the best antidote to langour.

I wished that I had a drop of your Loch Katrine water,[23] for our supply was neither cool nor over pure in this tropical clime; but it will have improved when we get south of the line, and into a more temperate latitude. As it is, we can render it very palatable by filtering, and the addition of a little lime juice and sugar.

The vessels which we saw yesterday were still visible. The Spaniard is only a short way ahead, very trifling after all the advantage that he had over us.

By eight o'clock in the evening a fine breeze had sprung up, and the ship sailed away before it.

Latitude 11° 0' N., longitude 24° 18' W. The temperature today was 82F.

23 July – The breeze stiffened during the night, and the ship rolled and got quite lively under us. In the morning the wind fortunately continued, and we went bowling along at eight knots. There had been a good deal of sickness and restlessness during the night, especially among the women and children between decks.

One boy this morning met with a severe fall on the deck, his legs having gone suddenly from him; he was taken up unconscious. A man also fell down the fore hatchway. Both were immediately tended by the surgeon, and, although considerably shaken, were not severely injured.

I saw my youngest daughter busy with the Latin verbs, our good friend of Trinity College, Dublin, having kindly volunteered to give her a lesson daily. While on the subject of language it was as well to remember that we have on board two well-informed young men from the Isle of Jersey, who have been accustomed from infancy to talk both English and French; but I think they were more partial to the latter language.

The temperature was 81F today, but the wind rendered the atmosphere very pleasant, especially as the sun had declined to shine, and at 12 o'clock noon the horizon darkened, and suddenly down came one of those tropical showers which soon deluge the decks. At the same time the sea rose, and the vessel rolled heavily. The change was very welcome to most of us, as it freshened the air, and besides, provided us with a plentiful supply of water.

We managed to fill all our casks, and tomorrow, if it was a fine day, would be devoted by many to washing. The rain had continued at intervals throughout the day, but not as violent as it had been earlier.

The ship was getting rapidly along, but, of course, our captain and officers have been unable to take their usual observations today. We were, however, in latitude 9° 15' N., longitude 23° 36' W., by dead reckoning. At ten o'clock at night the temperature was as high as 80F.

24 July –One of the most pleasant days we have had, in as far as a smart fresh breeze tempered the atmosphere, and gave speed to the ship.

A row of women stood on the deck actively engaged in washing. They have no verdant meadow on which to bleach their clothes, but they ascended to the skids, and spread their clothes out on the boats, where they dried under a tropical sun.

The wind was carrying us too far to the eastward; accordingly, as two and two do not always make four in the computations of our Chancellors of the Exchequer, so neither do eight knots by our log advance us anything like that distance on our proper course; on the contrary, not above three out of the eight could have been fairly carried to our credit.

A lady had been asking our third officer, a young sailor, how he had ever chosen the sea for his profession, and forsaken his own native Yorkshire. The beardless youth, pointing to the moon and the bright starry firmament, with the glad waters around, not forgetting the delicious softness of the air, remarked, 'Madam, did you ever experience such a lovely night on the land?' The lady admitted that she had not, but, at the same time, thought that the picture had another and a less alluring side.

Latitude 8° 22' N., longitude 21° 20' W., or about 560 miles off Sierra Leone. Temperature 81F in the shade.

25 July – We have had occasional showers today, that served to modify the temperature, which was 80F. There was still abundant perspiration amongst us, which, combined with the action of the sea air, covered our keys, pen-knives, and such articles of hardware on our persons, with a coating of rust.

We have reached latitude 6° 23' N., longitude 19° 27' W., and need not expect any further increase in the temperature, unless we get becalmed. This being Saturday night, a quiet little social circle was formed, and there was much pleasant chat.

26 July – Sunday, but no church services on deck. The vessel was rolling too much for that sort of work. The wind blew stiffly, not very favourably however, for we had to brace tightly.

During the morning the ship was put about, an operation which called forth all hands, including carpenter, cook, and sailmaker. We were now steering south and west, instead of south and east, as we have been doing for the last day or two, and which is so far for the better. A large barque had appeared sailing to eastward, but too distant to exchange numbers.

As Sunday was a comparatively quiet day with our sailors if the weather was moderate, I walked along to the forecastle this afternoon to see how Jack was spending his vacant hours.

Several were perusing their Bibles and other books. The boatswain, a regular old salt, was scanning the rigging intuitively, as if he could not direct his attention from the ship. Two young fellows who had served on board a man-of-war were going through the cutlass exercise with two short sticks. Another young sailor was intent upon reading one of the many works of our talented countryman, James Grant.[24]

Latitude 5° 40' N., longitude 18° 0' W., or about 340 miles from the equator. Temperature 80F.

27 July – A lovely day. We have had a raid into the forehold in quest of boxes, and it was very hot work. The [*Glasgow*] *Herald* printers' machine hall, when it was going full steam, was nothing in comparison.

The temperature was 81F, but in the evening it became comparatively cool and pleasant, with the ship going at 8½ knots.

Dancing commenced on the poop deck, and was kept up with great spirit, the motion of the vessel only seeming to lend additional zest to the quadrille and polka, as our fair ones tripped along the planks.

The exercise did bring out the perspiration, and the performers were glad of the interval allowed for refreshments in the saloon. Of course, the musicians soon cried out for their beer, as fiddling is a proverbially thirsty occupation, whether on sea or shore. It was rather an interesting spectacle to witness that homage to Terpsichore, far out in the Atlantic Ocean.

The forward passengers caught the contagion; having procured a concertina, they commenced their gambols on the quarter deck and all went joyous.

Latitude 3° 50' N., longitude 20° 50' W.

28 July – We were now nearing the line, and leaving the sun behind us. The temperature was lessening, as the thermometer stood only at 78F this morning. The wind had become more favourable, and we were advancing rapidly, and expected to cross the line tomorrow morning.

It was a really fine day; and one could not conceive more delightful weather, and yet, I dare say, if you had it in Buchanan Street in Glasgow, it would be deemed rather oppressive, as you have not passed through the ordeal which we have done, or became accustomed to go about so lightly clad.

In the afternoon there had been a sparring match on our poop deck between two of our young men, both tall and finely built Englishmen, and proficient in the art. It was a very graceful and animated encounter of skill.

We have had many beautiful nights at sea, but the general impression was that this evening had excelled them all. As the sun went down, it left the horizon illuminated with a bright glowing hue, and on turning to the westward, the moon sent forth a silver light.

No artist, not even Vernet,[25] the famous French marine painter, could have rendered such a lovely scene. There was such a purity and elasticity in the air, that one was loath to quit the deck.

Latitude 1° 5½' N., longitude 21° 33' W., or about 1,000 miles off Cape Palmas, nigh the Gold Coast [Ghana].

29 July, 12.30 p.m. – We will have crossed the line in half an hour hence, and it caused a little sensation on board. Some of the female passengers forward had been inquiring what the line meant, and what was to be seen. Jack in former days knew well that it meant a good deal of licence and boisterous merriment, and above all, a liberal allowance of grog.

But the world had become so circumspect in these more modern days, that the influence had extended to the ocean as well as to the land. The time honoured mystic rites were to be dispensed with, although the passengers were to make a contribution, in order provide some indulgence for our honest tars – and a fine manly lot they are.

I know not what form their jollification will take, for that depends on the pleasure of the captain, who is the monarch to us all for the time being, and I could not desire a more discreet and excellent ruler than Captain Thomas Funnell. I am well aware, however, that Jack would, if he was consulted, give the preference to rum, or something stiff, but I doubt he will be restricted to ale or stout.

The wind was blowing nicely in our direction today, and the fore studding sails were set, that we may reap the full advantage of the favouring gale. At 12 o'clock noon today we were in latitude 0° 4' N., longitude 23° 19' W., and our average speed has been from seven to eight knots.

30 July – We were now on the south of the line, and were well nigh becalmed. Accordingly, we felt the heat much more than if we had been in motion under a cooling breeze. Three articles of clothing, including light slippers, were quite sufficient, and if a cap or straw hat was added, it made a fourth.

Yesterday it was decided that our sailors should come aft, one by one, to the cuddy, and each get an allowance of beer or spirits, according to individual option, but on the express condition that the stuff should be consumed on the premises, and at night.

Jack took the huff at this arrangement, and preferred to get their tipple and carry it along to the forecastle. The result was that for the present they have gone without their grog, and no doubt considered themselves badly treated; it will, however, be doled out to them by degrees when they go off their watch.

The captain is wise in this restrictive policy. Looking to the good order and safety of the ship, I would rather see a keg of gunpowder than one of spirits go down the forecastle hatchway.

In the course of the evening the cabin passengers joined in the pastime of Blind Harry[26] on the poop deck, in the light of the moon. I was rather uneasy during its continuance, as the after companion was nearly on a level with the deck, and there was a risk of accident; but young people will be heedless.

I remembered a near relative of my own telling me that when serving in the *Vanguard* (80 guns), during the Syrian war,[27] his brother officers were on one occasion all joyfully engaged in a dance on the main deck, when one of the lieutenants forgot that the hatchway was behind him, and down he went, and was so fatally injured that he died in a very short time. To him it was 'the dance of death'.

We were now in the South Atlantic, latitude 1° 9' S., longitude 24° 9' W., and at about 11 o'clock at night a fine breeze fortunately started to blow.

31 July – We had been making throughout the night 7 knots, and the wind still served us, although it was lessening somewhat as we approached meridian. The temperature was 80F, which was rather pleasant if one kept out of the sun, and were sparing in the vestments.

A small whale was seen today, and also several gulls, who have found their way thus far out on the main, for we are hundreds of miles from any land, being in latitude 2° 28' S., longitude 25° 9' W., or nearer to Cape St. Roque, in South America, than Cape Palmas in Africa. The Isle of Ascension was the nearest adjacent land, but we were far distant even from it.

Our young men had been amusing themselves by going up the rigging. One or two ascended to the cross-jack yard, hand over hand, and were well satisfied with the feat, when suddenly our first officer caught hold of the rope, and mounted and descended with an ease and celerity that laughed to scorn all the efforts of our amateurs. His name is Mr. Thomas Woolley, who was deservedly respected by all on board.

He possessed a short, firmly-knit frame – might pass for 35 years of age, though he is only 25, so weatherbeaten were his features and so grave was his deportment – ever alive to his responsibilities, and ever constant to his duties.

One of our young men ascended as far as the mizzen royals, and was about to come down by their halyards, when he was timeously warned by the second officer to descend as he went up, or by the standing rigging, and eschew the halyards or running rigging.

While I was sitting at the time reading in the saloon, I observed the eyes of those standing at the stern directed aloft, and on going up the companion to see what was going on, to my surprise I beheld my own little chap well nigh up to the mizzen top, which he had gained by shinning, or plying feet and hands on two ropes about a foot and a half apart.

When Buchanan moved from Edinburgh to Glasgow with his surviving family during the late 1850s, he resided at fashionable St George's Road, near to St George's Cross. This 1839 sketch (part of the feuing plan of the lands of Southpark) was penned at the time when the west end area of Glasgow was being laid out for accommodation to suit the growing, wealthy middle class of the city who were benefiting financially and materially from the growth of Glasgow into the 'second city of the empire'. When Buchanan moved into the west end, the development of the area had been in progress for around 20 years. Courtesy of Glasgow City Council Archives

Of course I did not shout up to him to come down, and, perhaps scare him, but let him quietly descend, and then told him to desist from those pranks in future, though I doubt if he will rigidly adhere to my orders. The truth is, that I was prone to do the same things myself at his age.

---

1. Arran is a large island situated in the Firth of Clyde on the Scottish west coast, often referred to as Scotland in miniature.

2. The 'little fellow' is Buchanan's son Robert, who was 11 years old at the time of the voyage.

3. The Bay of Biscay lies to the south-west of the French Atlantic coast.

4. Dumbarton Castle is situated upon a large volcanic rock near the town of Dumbarton, on the estuary of the River Leven, where it flows into the River Clyde. It was the scene of a Viking siege against local forces in the eleventh century AD.

5. The Broomielaw was the harbour in the centre of Glasgow, from where shipping services to the ports on the Clyde estuary departed. Millport, Rothesay and Dunoon are towns on the island of Great Cumbrae, the island of Bute, and the Cowal peninsula respectively, all popular holiday destinations at the time.

6. James Fenimore Cooper, an American author who lived 1789–1851 and was famous for his stories of the sea. His most famous novel was *The Last of the Mohicans*.

7. Frederick Marryat 1792–1848, an English naval officer and novelist, who wrote *Mr Midshipman Easy*, and was also famous for his children's stories.

8. A quotation from 'The Lass o' Gowrie', by the songwriter Carolina Nairne (1766–1845), meaning, 'A little while before the sun went down.'

9. At that time Trinity College was a prestigious seat of learning in Dublin, Ireland, which was then part of the United Kingdom.

10. 'Fancy work' refers to handiwork such as knitting and crochet.

11. 'Mother Cary's chickens' is maritime slang for the stormy petrel seabird.

12. The Western Isles are the Hebridean and other islands off the west coast of Scotland.

13. Barrhead was a town in East Renfrewshire, to the south-west of Glasgow.

14. Although Buchanan notes this as a line from a work by English poet John Dryden (1631–1730), he was in error as it is quoted as an epigram in Sir Walter Scott's *The Monastery*, at the beginning of Chapter 10, and is attributed to Robert Dekker (?1570–1662).

15. Tom Coffin was a character created by James Fenimore Cooper. See note 6 above.

16. A type of fishing vessel that was frequently found around the Canadian Newfoundland coast during the 19th century.

17. William Cobbett, 1763–1835, English-born writer and champion of the poor. He resided for several spells in the USA, including farming on Long Island in 1817–19, and became MP for Oldham in England in 1832. In the early 1800s he wrote the celebrated *Rural Rides*, a book describing the decline of the living conditions of the rural labourers in southern England.

18. The *Scotsman* became a leading newspaper in Scotland during the 19th century and has rivalled the *Glasgow Herald* [*The Herald*], up until the present day. It bought out and absorbed the *Caledonian Mercury*, once an employer of David Buchanan, in 1867.

19. General Robert E. Lee, commander of the Confederate forces during the American Civil War.

20. These were luminaries of the Scottish law courts at the Court of Session in Edinburgh. The residences noted were to the south of the city.

21. A position to the south of what is today the Canary Islands, and to the west of modern-day Western Sahara.

22. Given the position quoted by Buchanan, the group of islands referred to would be the Santo Antão group of the Cape Verde islands, several hundred miles off the west coast of Senegal in north-west Africa.

23. Loch Katrine, located in the area of central Scotland commonly known as the Trossachs, had been developed as the water supply for the city of Glasgow by the late 1850s.

24. James Grant of Corrimony, 1743–1835. He was born in Inverness-shire and educated at Edinburgh University, becoming an advocate in 1767. He also pursued a literary career and in 1813 he published *Thoughts on the Origin and Descent of the Gael.* His opposition to the government of the time was believed to have prevented him from gaining an official position within the Scottish legal establishment.

25. Claude Joseph Vernet, 1714–89, French landscape and marine painter. The Louvre in Paris exhibited his sixteen paintings of France's main seaports, which had been commissioned by the French King Louis XIV.

26. A game in which a participant is blindfolded, probably similar to the game of blind man's buff.

27. The Syrian War that is referred to would have been what is more commonly known as the Turko-Egyptian wars of 1832–33 and 1839–41. Egypt invaded Syria in 1832 and Russia entered the conflict on the side of the Turks. Britain and France became alarmed at the Russian involvement, and after a few years of confusion Egypt was attacked by the Turks in Syria in 1839. The Turks were repulsed after the Egyptian victory at the Battle of Nezib. Britain and Austria then intervened, and a combined naval force bombarded and captured Beirut and Acre during October and November 1840. British Admiral Charles Napier oversaw an agreement whereby Egypt abandoned claims to Syria, and evacuated the country in 1841.

August 1863

1 August – The wind had been brisk during the night, and favourable. This morning at six o'clock our speed was 10 knots, and we were now in the forenoon counting eight knots, the motion having been remarkably smooth. In the evening it blew stiffly, and we began to plough through the water at a fast rate.

It was Saturday night at sea, and they were rather noisy in the fore part. Two big fellows were sparring by the light of the moon.

I had a quiet and very pleasant chat with our captain and Captain Marshall, late of HM 36th Infantry, a most agreeable, well-informed man, who has seen service in various parts of the world. He goes to New Zealand for his health.

Latitude 4° 12' S., longitude 26° 1' W.

2 August – Sunday morning and we had a strong breeze, but too much from the south for our benefit. At eight o'clock in the morning our speed was 10½ knots, and the ship rolled, although not violently.

In the afternoon, while we were sitting quietly at the dessert, something that was going on forward caught the eye of the captain as he was sitting at the head of the table. He immediately started up, and not being able to put aside his chair quickly enough, as it was lashed to the table, as it was in its turn to the floor, he bounded over the back of it and rushed along the poop gangway.

It proved to be a fight, or rather melee. As I subsequently learned, a few of the intermediate passengers had clubbed for a liberal allowance of sherry, which they had consumed rather rapidly and it had them in a drunken state. One tall young Irishman had offended a little smart Englishman, when the latter let fly at his opponent, who then retaliated, and knocked down the small man. He got up, however, and struck out again, when he was floored once more. Another party then interfered, when the little man, apparently none the worse for his falls, turned upon the newcomer and hit him down.

Two Scotchmen from the fore hatchway then mingled in the fight; but at this stage the captain arrived on the scene and in a moment quelled the brawl. It was rather an unseemly exhibition, and especially on a Sunday afternoon.

The little fellow to whom I have alluded did not appear to be of a quarrelsome nature, but, on the contrary, cheerful and obliging. His opponent, the Irishman, is also a very frank, honest, good-hearted fellow. The Englishman had, however, conceived himself insulted, and his blood had got up.

They threaten to have it out when they get on land if not before, but this I believed to be vain talk. A ship was a bad place for a simmering quarrel, as the hostile parties were always coming in each other's way.

Latitude 6° 51' S., longitude 27° 39' W., which showed a long run since yesterday.

3 August – It continued to blow very stiffly from the south, although we were now in a region where we might have expected the south-east trade winds. We were going at a rate of 10 knots, but, unfortunately, for every one mile we proceeded in the right direction we went four miles in the wrong.

As Mr. Woolley, the first officer, remarked to me, 'It is a hard-hearted wind,' but we were tearing along under it, and it had brought us within about 350 miles, or less than two days sail, of Pernambuco [Recife], on the South American coast. The distance traversed since yesterday had been 330 miles, which showed what the *Ganges* could do when she had got a wind.

Today was the birthday of a fine young Englishman, a landed proprietor in Wiltshire, who was very popular with us all, for he was a really good fellow, and there was a special libation on the occasion. The captain proposed his health and many happy returns and so forth. Our host, for such he was on the auspicious day, responded with excellent humour and good taste.

The ladies were duly honoured, and also the Church of England, coupled with the name of, and in deference to, our respected friend of Trinity College. In short, all were as merry as good fellowship, and harmless pleasantry could make a party of people, careering along the South Atlantic. There would have been a dance in the evening, but there were two obstacles, viz., the want of moonlight, and the rather heavy rolling of the ship.

Latitude 9° 23' S., longitude 30° 29' W. Temperature 79F.

4 August – The wind was strong and steady, but rather more favourable than yesterday. During the night the log gave 12 knots, which is the highest rate we have as yet attained.

At seven o'clock in the morning we met a homeward-bound vessel, and managed to signal our number. We then signalled to report having seen us, but no response was hoisted, as the vessels were passing each other too quickly for further talk. We suspected the ship was for England, and, if so, we may be heard of at home about the end of September.

Today at noon we had reached latitude 12° 48' S., longitude 32° 53' W., and had run 235 miles since yesterday, which made a southing of 205 miles. That was excellent work, considering that the ship was going close hauled.

At six o'clock at night a dark cloud appeared to windward, when suddenly there came a squall, and the ship which, ten minutes previously, when the log was hove, was going at 7½ knots, seemed to rush forward as it swept the foam from its bows. The wind soon moderated, but we had fitful gusts, with rain, during the night. As I heard the rain pattering on the planks above my berth, it conveyed a sensation of great snugness. Temperature, 80F.

5 August – A fine morning, with a good wind, and the motion pretty smooth in the circumstances. The deck forward was like a village green, with the children playing in all directions. Some of them had got a rope attached to a box, in which they were pulling each other about. Poor things, they appeared very merry, and it is wonderful to see what good sea legs some of the most tiny urchins of two and three years of age have acquired.

During the night there had been a sharp matrimonial squall below. From what I have heard it was an affair that would have done no discredit to certain localities in Glasgow.

In the morning we met a vessel apparently bound for the Brazilian coast. We signalled, but do not know whether we succeeded in conveying our number, and we could not at the distance make out that of our neighbour.

Latitude 5° 42' S., longitude 32° 51' W., which gave a southing of 174 geographical miles, and an easting of two, which was not a bad day's work, and, moreover, all in the right direction. Temperature, 79F.

6 August – This was a lovely day, but I may well ask what days did not come under that category, for we have became so accustomed to sunshine that we seemed to expect nothing else. Scarcely a breath of wind stirred; the sails flapped lazily against the masts, and the ship gently rocked on the heave of the ocean. But we may have a different tale to tell when we get farther south, and commence to round the Cape of Good Hope.

I had a good talk last night with Mr. William Valentine, our second officer, about old Scotland. He is an Aberdonian, but is connected, as I am myself, with the Howe of the Mearns.[1] We discovered that we had a number of mutual and esteemed friends among the worthy farmers at the foot of the Grampians, and could recall many pleasant associations with that beautiful district.

Towards night it commenced to rain, and the wind came, which gradually quickened until it blew a rather stiff gale. Sail had in consequence to be taken in and furled.

Latitude 17° 15' S., longitude 32° 22' W. The temperature at 1 p.m. was 81F.

7 August – It had blown a great deal during the night, and several were complaining during the morning of want of rest. I heard one female address another – 'How did you sleep during the storm?' If they consider what we had last night as coming up to a storm, I suspect they will be rather amazed at what they will very probably experience when they get into a different latitude.

It was a fine day, although still blowing, and more against us than for us. The wind was, however, moderating, but we had no royals and skysails set today. The temperature was very pleasant, the thermometer being only 76F, which is lower than it had been for nearly a month.

Little work had been done by the good ship *Ganges* for the last 24 hours, as we had only made latitude 18° 11' S., longitude 33° 9' W. We were less than 300 miles from Porto Alegre, in Brazil, and about 180 miles from the small, and, I believe, uninhabited Isle of Trinidade, in the South Atlantic.[2]

8 August – The sun had not shone forth today, and the wind blew very softly; we do not want it stronger, as it is not friendly, and would take us farther west when our course now lay south-east, with a view to round the Cape. The thermometer at 9 a.m. had stood at 73F in the captain's cabin, so that I fear we will soon be complaining that it was too cool with an eager nip in the air.

During the morning we were greeted by a Cape pigeon, which came so near that we could distinguish its varied plumage. We may expect more of such visitants, and might have a chance of capturing one or two, though they would prove a rather tough, oily morsel, and scarcely find their way to the cook's galley unless we were sore pressed as to provisions; of which there is as yet little prospect.

It is true our hen and duck coops now present a beggarly show as compared with that day (23rd June) when our bower anchor was brought home off Gravesend. But the consolation is that those feathered bipeds would die a natural death unless our butcher saved them that trouble; they grew thin with the tossing about, and rejected their food, confined as they were.

They say in our country that it was difficult to take a certain garment off a Highlandman. So I can testify from practical experience that it was equally so to get a nice morsel out of the breast of our *Ganges* ducks. Let the poultry, therefore, go the way of all flesh as speedily as they may; the solace remained that we have still nearly three-fourths of our sheep and pigs to the fore, besides preserved meats and other good things galore. As for water, we were in no lack, as in addition to our casks, the *Ganges* possessed an iron tank, which reached from the kelson to the main deck, and which has a capacity of upwards of 4,000 gallons.

Today happened to be the birthday of the amiable consort of our excellent, respected young surgeon, and it has been duly celebrated. Wine and cake have been served around the saloon; but, if the truth must be told, the majority of our young men preferred the sherry. The consequence was that the cabin was very joyous, and I could scarcely get my own little man to sit down to his task, though it was not too heavy for his youthful shoulders.

At about nine o'clock at night, as I was sitting in the saloon, I saw the captain step into the first officer's cabin and come forth with a pair of manacles, which indicated something wrong in the forward part of the ship.

It turned out that one of the cook's mates – an Irishman who had already displayed a turbulent disposition – had managed by some clandestine means to get drunk, and was threatening violence to those around. At the sight of the captain, however, he became quiet, and appeared to go peaceably down to his berth below.

This proved to be a delusive calm, for the fellow soon after appeared with a knife in his hand, swearing and vowing vengeance against all in general, and some one or two in particular.

There was, of course, a regular commotion, in the midst of which the captain rushed forward and got him secured, but not before he had wounded one man, a Scotchman, on the wrist and face, though fortunately not seriously.

He was immediately placed in irons, and carried aft to the poop deck, on which he was lashed to a ring bolt, and laid for the night under a sail.

When the deck was quiet, none but the officer on watch being upon it, I chanced to go up, and I passed my hand across his hot forehead. He was breathing hard, as might be expected, after his debauch.

Latitude 19° 13' S., longitude 34° 30' W.

9 August – Another lovely Sunday morning with a temperature of 75F at nine o'clock. Between six and seven a.m. I looked out; the culprit from yesterday was still on the poop deck. He raised up his manacled hands and gave a look up, and then lay down with his face flat on the deck – and an ill-favoured face it was, besides being bruised and disfigured.

At eight o'clock the captain ordered the male steerage passengers to assemble in front of the poop, when he addressed them in a very frosty fashion, as to the occurrence of the preceding evening. Although there was still a calm demeanour about him.

As nearly as I can recollect he thus delivered himself – 'Well, I have brought you all forward here in consequence of the turbulence that took place last night. It is evident to my mind, that the man who got drunk and threatened to stab two or three persons, must have done so by some of you having given him liquor out of your private stores, as there was no other way that he could have got it.

'It is the rule that no such private stock should be brought on board; but thinking that I had a responsible lot of characters about me, I did not wish to proceed to make a rigorous search of your luggage when we were off Gravesend.

'None of the crew can get grog by any other means, and as it is the first time that many of you may have been at sea, you may not think of the consequences to which such a proceeding may lead.

'But I may warn you, that it was about four years ago, and very near to where we now are, that the *Eastern City*, a ship containing nearly the same number on board as now are in the *Ganges*, took fire through a similar occurrence as we had last night. In all probability, every soul on board that ship, the *Eastern City*, would have perished, had it not been for a ship that I was in, coming to the rescue and saving all on board. Providentially for them, the ship that I was in had been driven considerably out of its regular course.

'Now mind what I say – for I never say what I do not intend to perform – that if another incidence of drunkenness occurs on board, I shall order that not a drop of beer or spirits shall be sold to any soul on board; and thus all will be brought to suffer through the fault of one or two reckless individuals.

'It is a saying that, "when they know nothing they fear nothing," and therefore none of you can say what will happen if liquor is put in the way of some madcap.

'It fortunately happened differently with the *Ganges* last night from what it did with the *Eastern City*; but there is no reason why it might not have been the same. If any of you at a time wish to give a glass of grog to any of the crew, I do not object, provided that it is done through the purser, for that is the only way in which it can be done.

'Another matter I wish to mention to you is, that I have seen, when walking along the poop, fire flying about as you were lighting your pipes. Now, nothing can be more dangerous in these tropical climes, as everything about a ship becomes as dry as tinder.

'I therefore trust that you will all attend to what I have now said, for it may be, that if I find another instance of any one thus offending, the party will not land at Auckland as a free man, but under arrest.'

This address, under the circumstances, was received with marked approbation, and I hope will have a salutary effect.

A party was then brought forward and charged with having given the spirits to the cook's mate; he of course denied the impeachment, and the proof could not be obtained. The culprit was lodged in the fore sick bay, not only manacled, but also fettered, for he was evidently a character who, for the present at least, must not be let loose.

The person who was wounded was doing well, no thanks to the cook's mate. He knocked his assailant down twice in self-defence, the second time after he was wounded in the wrist.

Latitude 21° 37' S., longitude 34° 56' W.

10 August – The wind had been fair throughout the night, and the ship had been making good progress; but towards morning the horizon became overcast, and we had a copious shower of rain, which refreshed the atmosphere. The thermometer stood at 73F in the morning, which showed that we were bidding adieu to the hot weather.

The cook's mate had been released from his irons this morning, but he was disrated, and would no more enter the galley. I saw him along with the sailors and pulling at the braces, for he will now take his watch.

There is a shrewd belief that he had been too familiar with penal treatment, as when they were clapping the irons upon him, he wisely made no struggle, knowing well that it would be in vain, and he would only aggravate his troubles.

He also, immediately after he was incarcerated, threw himself into the most comfortable position, as if he knew how to find it. If he caused any fresh disturbance, he would be kept in irons for the remainder of the voyage, and sent ashore a prisoner; as he himself knows. He is berthed beneath the forecastle, nigh the quarters of that worthy old growler, the boatswain.

Latitude 23° 52' S., longitude 33° 56' W., or upwards of 500 miles off Rio de Janeiro.

11 August – A beautiful day, with the thermometer at 73F. The air is so perfect, that some have said they desired no change, at least for nine months in the year. We had a fine wind during last night, and have been forging along at from 9 to 10 knots.

What a contrast the weather presented in comparison with some of those fogs that I have seen overcome the city of Glasgow. I especially recollect one memorable tract of murky weather, which occurred at the beginning of 1860, when the hours of daylight were assisted with gaslight, and it was difficult to find one's way from street to street.

I saw the boatswain busily superintending the removal of the spare spars from the top of the round house situated in the waist of the ship, and lashing the same to the deck. The roof was now clear of all dead weight, save the longboat, under which some live weight, or three collie dogs, belonging to our doughty friend the Yorkshire farmer, have been located since the commencement of the voyage. He said that he would not take 'a hoondred poond' for them. I think he will be spared a refusal, although I do not doubt he has made a good investment in the transport of those sagacious, useful animals.

The object of the nether stowage of the spars was, of course, to make the ship all taut for a blow that may be expected one of those days.

The wise counsel given by our captain on Sunday morning has not fallen like water spilled on the ground. The male passengers in the midships and forehatch cabins have constituted, of course with the cordial sanction of the captain, a committee of public safety, and two of them take watch by rotation during the night, so that if anything untoward occurred between decks the circumstance would be immediately reported to the officer on watch on deck.

One or two Irishmen declined to go into the movement, alleging that there was no occasion for it. Perhaps they rather preferred a scuffle now and then, firmly believing that a well-regulated community, whether on sea or shore, was all the better for an occasional squall. At all events, the committee could dispense with such reluctant coadjutors when choosing who were to be appointed guardians of the night.

Latitude 26° 17' S., longitude 31° 25' W., or an excellent day's work.

12 August – We must now be into the south-east trades, as the wind had blown very steady throughout the night, and we were going at fully nine knots.

Various devices are resorted to on a long voyage to while away the time. Some of our young men have constructed a kite, which was let off today from the mizzen top, and formed a very pretty object as it was seen flying above the waters, while a Cape pigeon disported in the vicinity. The forward passengers had a raffle yesterday for a concertina, and today subscribers, including most of the cabin passengers, are coming forward to have a raffle for a gun.

The thermometer stood at 72F this morning, which was very agreeable. When the sun set, about half past five o'clock this evening, it felt rather cold, and at a later period those who chose to remain on deck had their garments saturated with the heavy dew.

Our young Englishmen had been cleaning their fowling pieces, rifles, and revolvers, but there was no grouse shooting for them this day, although hundreds of their countrymen would have been blazing away on the moors of Caledonia.

Latitude 28° 14' S., longitude 29° 32' W.

13 August – At 11 o'clock forenoon the temperature was 71F, and the atmosphere was positively delightful, so balmy and so pure. The wind was also fair, and the ship carried a cloud of sail, both studding and stay sails having been set. Our last log gave eight knots.

The motion, however, is quite smooth, so that we might forget we were far out on the South Atlantic, were it not that, when we open the cabin door we must not let it go, or it will go bang-bang until secured; and when I was in the bath today the water went swaying to and fro, never at rest for a moment.

I saw our sheep running on deck; they had been taken out of their pens by way of an airing and a little exercise. The doctor was inspecting them, but I have a shrewd guess that our Yorkshire farmer would be more competent for that task, as it was more in his line.

When his shepherd dogs spotted the sheep from the top of the round house, they immediately started barking, as if they were once more on *terra firma*, and about to resume their usual vocation. One sheep would not get up on her legs, when one fellow said comically that, 'The animal ought to be killed to save its life.' They were driving them in a flock round the mainmast; and they would be the better for that rousing.

Latitude 29° 36' S., longitude 26° 45' W.

14 August – A fine breeze, with the thermometer down to 68F at nine o'clock this morning, when our rate was 9½ knots; in the course of the night we reached 11 knots. The ship rolled a little, but we clapped on additional sail, so as to give the wind not the chance of an escape from every inch of duck that could be rendered available.

At two o'clock, as I stood on the forecastle, I saw a long dark streak stretching along the southern horizon, which indicated a squall. The boatswain shook his head in the direction, as much as to say, 'I know what you're after.'

Immediately after, the order was given to 'stand by the halyards'; then came the wind and the rain, and all hands were alive in taking down the studding sails. The wind had suddenly veered to the south, and the ship had to be laid on to it, or her course changed from south-east to north-east, until the sails were taken in. It became very cold, and pilot coats were in requisition.

The night was gusty, but we contrived to make ourselves very comfortable in the cuddy, with the after companion door shut. For the first time since we were out of the English Channel I hugged the blanket.

No doubt, when my boy and I lay down at night as we were going through the tropics, we made a fashion of going below a thin coverlet, and blanket, being to the manner born; when we awakened in the morning, however, we generally found ourselves scudding under bare poles, although our port was always kept open throughout the night, as indeed it still was, with the exception of a small bit of the Venetian blind up.

Latitude 30° 29' S., longitude 22° 58' W.

15 August – The wind continued unfavourable, and was driving us east by north half north. It was cold, the thermometer being as low as 66F at nine o'clock a.m. As we have to keep well up to the wind, the spray was flying over the forecastle and waist of the ship. I heard shouts of laughter as some unlucky soul received a ducking on the way from the galley with his pie.

A flock of Cape pigeons were flying in our wake; pretty creatures they are, and welcome too, being the only signs of animated nature within the compass of our vision. Some were making attempts to capture them by means of a long line with a hook upon which was a piece of pork. One did bite and broke the hook.

As the evening came, the wind rose, and we surged along at from nine to ten knots, but unfortunately we were driven north by north-east, or in a very contrary direction from that which we wished to go. The ship rolled, but still there was little difficulty in pacing the deck, provided one set doggedly to the task.

It was Saturday night, and people carried the associations of land and home along with them on the sea; but remembering the events of the preceding Saturday, the captain and purser kept a sharp look out as to what was going on between decks. Not a drop of beer or stout was given out after nine o'clock in the evening, although there were numerous and urgent applications.

As the purser remarked to me, several would return to their quarters and say, 'There is not a chance, for that blasted purser was sitting in the saloon close to the door of the steward's pantry.' But there is nothing like order on board a ship, as I am happy to say it was now on board the *Ganges*, while such external dangers as rocks, winds, and waves, had to be encountered as best as possible.

Latitude 30° 5' S., longitude 19° 25' W.

16 August – It still blows, and too much against us. This morning the thermometer stood at 64F.

During the quiet, bright weather which we had while in the tropics, as the bell tolled for the morning worship forward, I could have fancied myself in some of our quiet moorland parishes, if I could have shut out the surrounding scene, a blue above and a blue below, a blue everywhere. The illusion was further heightened by a number of lonely Scotch voyagers who quietly awaited the arrival of the minister.

What a contrast today presented in the costume as compared with the last and preceding hot Sundays! On the seventh day there was always some effort made by nearly all on board, including the sailors while off the watch, to amend their apparel. But this was done tropically.

I have seen crimson and white the predominant colours among all manner of dress, and I fancied that some of us would rather have attracted attention if we had been seen to exit thus from the Ramshorn Kirk,[3] which was the last resting place of that fine old Glasgow gentleman of former years, yclept Captain Paton[4] who, according to the local song, mixed ambrosial punch with limes that 'on his property in Trinidad did grow'.

Still, dress was all a matter of custom and association. One night for example, by way of an innocent lark, I went on deck with an ordinary hat, and all around looked as if they had witnessed an apparition, for such an article was never visible on board. For my part, I trust that I may never be condemned to wear one of those ugly inconvenient things in the future.

Someone blessed the man who invented sleep, but I don't think the same charity ought to be extended to him, whoever he was, that taught Englishmen to put such chimney-pots on their heads. I believe that dress, and how it was viewed by the onlooker, all depended upon other people and their surroundings.

I recollected once having read a very interesting book by a Russian voyager who had visited the South Sea Islands. He repaired once to a church on an island where there was a missionary settlement. On entering, he was taken aback by the quite outlandish rig of some of the native converts, who had conceived themselves the beau ideal of fashion if they could lay hold of any stray cast-off European clothing.

One figure in particular struck him. It was a tall, raw-boned, converted savage, who stood in a most devout attitude, with nothing to cover nature save a faded, tattered sergeant's coat, which he had managed to procure. In this garb he strutted, the envy of his countrymen. He was much in the predicament of Marryat's[5] Boatswain Briggs, who, when Midshipman Easy mislaid his nether vestments while on shore, was compelled to report himself on the quarter deck in that state. 'Are you sober?' said the captain. 'Perfectly sober, sir; but I have lost my trousers.' The boatswain's maxim as to others was duty before decency; but he little knew that it would be tested one day on himself.

Some on board were apt to forget that it was 'Soonday', as my Yorkshire friends call it. I saw one of our sailors sitting comfortably under the forecastle deftly darning his

The last piece of British soil that David Buchanan and his family stood upon was the pier at Tilbury where they boarded a small vessel that took them out to the Ganges, moored off Gravesend on the opposite bank of the River Thames. This view c.1887 shows the Tilbury hotel and pier from the Gravesend bank of the river with sailing ships still prominently moored in midstream. Courtesy of the University of St. Andrews Library

stockings. Poor Jack! I daresay that he would plead in extenuation that he could not find a leisure hour on any of the six legitimate days.[6]

A large flock of Cape pigeons and other aquatic birds were gliding about on our stern. Sometimes they suddenly and simultaneously squat themselves on the water, as if they were proceeding to hold a council of war, to decide whether or not they would board us and attempt to take the ship.

Now, I well remember to have heard old Cobbett,[7] in one of his many tirades against the game laws, thus deliver himself: 'It is instinctive in man to kill or capture the wild animal that he sees running at his feet. Lord bless you, ladies and gentlemen, even churchmen form no exception to this universal law of nature, for you must understand that the Right Reverend Father in God, the Lord Bishop of Durham, is very fond of field sports.'

I presume that it was some such instinct that had brought a party of young men aft to the taffrail, where they were eagerly engaged with their lines in endeavouring to catch those birds. At length a young Irishman succeeded in hooking one and bringing it on board. Of course the event excited a considerable sensation when the bird was taken down and exhibited on the main deck. An albatross was also seen, which would have measured several feet between the tips of the wings.

We were today in latitude 28° 29' S., longitude 17° 10' W., which was an untoward result for we had been driven back by the strong head wind far to the north-westward, or the very reverse of the direction we should have been going, which was to the south-east.

17 August – We have had a quiet night, and this morning there was scarcely a breath of wind stirring, but what blew was more favourable. Still the yards were sharply braced up. The thermometer was at 65F at nine o'clock in the morning.

Two more Cape pigeons had been caught, and our young fellows were all intent on the sport. The sailors were occupied in bending new and strong sails, in anticipation of coarse weather some of these days.

As the day advanced we got becalmed and lay like a log on the water. An empty hamper, which looks very like as if it had contained champagne, was seen floating at a little distance. It had probably been thrown overboard from a vessel, which we have seen a good way ahead of us for the last few days.

A slight breeze sprang up at night, and we made six knots to the southward, but our course lay to the south-east; however, we were thankful for small mercies, considering the recent wayward conduct of our ship. We were today in latitude 29° 36' S., longitude 17° 8' W., so that we were still engaged in making up the way we had lost, having been driven back from latitude 30° 29' S., which we had reached three days ago.

18 August – We had been eight weeks at sea today, and on the whole had much reason to be grateful for the weather and comfort which we had hitherto enjoyed.

Today we had a nice fair breeze, and, as nearly as I could judge, must have been making about seven knots in the right direction. The thermometer, at 11 o'clock, stood at 67½F. It was more like one of those fine autumnal days which we occasionally have in Scotland, than any weather that we had experienced during the voyage. Studding sails were set above and below, and towards the afternoon the breeze freshened, which sent the ship dashing along at eight knots.

A rainbow appeared, being the second we had seen during the voyage. My young friend who caught one of the Cape pigeons yesterday, had skinned and stuffed the bird in a very skilful, artistic manner.

Latitude 30° 21' S., longitude 15° 20' W.

19 August – There was a fine fair wind today, and the ship sailed along very jauntily. We had, however, a considerable swell, and it caused the *Ganges* to rock.

It required a little dexterity in the morning to wield my razor. But there is nothing like determination to do a thing, and then it will be done, although shaving is a department of the toilet with which the vast majority on board have dispensed with.

The rolling of the ship had caused several falls among some who had forgotten to keep their weather-eye open, and attempt to humour the vessel. I saw one of the strongest men among the cabin passengers suddenly spreadeagled full length on the deck. He was out in the Crimea during the war, having been attached, I believe, to the railway or navvie brigade, and he assisted with the construction of the gabions[8] that were used in the siege of Sebastapol. I heard him just now ordering a bottle of stout, as his athletic frame seemed to receive no shock from the tumble.

Overhead, I listened to the sharp, decided tread of the captain, pacing backwards and forwards, as regularly as a recruiting sergeant marching up and down in front of the Tontine.[9] The ship gave one roll, when the lower stern-sail boom went down as if it was going to dip into the water, and when the counter heave came it pointed aloft. How she rolls at this moment!

I then heard a noise outside, within a few yards of me. It proved to be a heave of the ship, which had upset a family, as they were seated in front of the poop. Stools and occupants all went on the run.

It had become so troublesome daily, to regulate our watches according to the proper time, as indicated by the observations of the course of the sun, that most of us had given up the task. As long as we were going westward from Greenwich we had of course to put our watches forward with the ship's clock, and now that we are going eastward, we had to reverse the procedure.

As any elementary work would explain, 15 degrees east or west makes an hour of difference in the time, as compared with that at Greenwich – *i.e.*, the circumference of the globe was 360 degrees, which, divided by the 24 hours, or period of the daily revolution of the earth, gives a figure of 15.

Thus, if we journey 15 degrees west of Greenwich, it will be 11 o'clock when it is 12 o'clock at Greenwich; and, on the other hand, if our course takes us 15 degrees east from Greenwich, it will be in the meridian of the ship one o'clock when it is only noon in the meridian of Greenwich, because the sun has passed over that point, eastward, one hour before it has done so at Greenwich.

If, then, the sun takes the hour to traverse 15 degrees of the circumference of the globe, it requires 4 minutes, or the 15th part of 60 minutes, to accomplish one degree, or 60 geographical miles; and if 4 minutes or 240 seconds, are divided by 60, it gives one mile to every four seconds. Of course, this does not affect the multitude who toil at their daily occupations on shore, as few of them give any heed to it.

The swell rises as the day advanced, and shouts of laughter were heard as any mishap occurred, which showed that the passengers had become pretty well seasoned, after having been two months now away from dry land.

But if one could imagine 300 passengers on board one of the Clyde river steamers suddenly brought into our position, you would witness a very different scene, and I can imagine that the cries of discomfort and distress would predominate over the sounds of laughter and merriment.

The swell was upon our stern, and affected us the more because our course compelled us to keep our yards square, and, moreover, we were light, our deadweight being at the bottom of the ship, and the space between decks occupied with passengers, instead of being filled up with cargo.

When two o'clock p.m. (the cabin dinner-hour) came, there were a few mischances before the dishes could be rightly settled down. A dish of haricots opposite to me, gave a violent sway to my side, and flooded my plate with gravy; at the succeeding or counter roll it paid the like homage to my neighbour, a fair young Essex lady. A roast of mutton before the captain behaved in the same unmannerly style. Withal, our company managed to do ample justice to the vivres [victuals]. When it became dark there was no abatement of the swell as it was rather on the rise.

Latitude 31° 26' S., longitude 13° 5' W.; therefore, when it was ten o'clock a.m. with us today, it was 11.24 and 44 seconds a.m. back in Glasgow, or a difference of 35 minutes and 16 seconds – the city being in longitude 4° 16' W. of Greenwich. Temperature 67F.

20 August – It was a trite saying, that when some were very fatigued they could sleep without rocking. If such people had been on board the *Ganges* last night, they would have slept doubly sound, for we were rocked in fine style.

The swell continued, and we rolled to and fro; if it was on our bow instead of the stern we would pitch, which I would prefer to rolling, though neither discomposed me in any great degree. The day is otherwise fine and we went along at 10½ knots. There was no abatement of the swell; and we rolled heavily.

When dinner came, there was the same difficulty as yesterday in getting things to remain steady. Every article had to be secured, or it would go adrift, and there was such a creaking of the timbers.

I had to hold my soup plate in my hand, and raise and depress it with the motion of the vessel, otherwise the fluid would have gone into my lap instead of to its proper destination.

At tea time (six o'clock p.m.) the wind had got slightly on the starboard quarter, and there was a corresponding change in the yards, which were swung a little way round. This eased the ship in some degree, although we still had to steady ourselves.

As I was reading in the saloon, seated in the chair of the doctor, who was the vice-president of our mess, it had to be lashed to the cabin table on both sides, and I felt that if either of the marline lashings snapped, the chair and its occupant would hurl downward into the corner – which fate, indeed, befell me on one occasion, when I had not taken the precaution of making my seat fast.

As for my vestments, I make according to use and wont, suspend them in my cabin on going to bed, but I find them strewed on the floor in the morning. Last night I thought it as well to toss them down at once, knowing that I would find everything higgledy-piggledy in the morning. The solace was that nothing could run far away.

One might imagine that, our dimensions being so limited at sea, everything would be ready and handy, and at all times within our reach; and such might be the case if we were only trotting up and down the Clyde from Rothesay to the Broomielaw;[10] but out here we were never sure of finding a thing where we placed it, for nothing remained at rest unless regularly fastened; and even while in that state, it was ever threatening to break loose.

One may as well search for a needle in a hayrick as for any small article that had gone amissing when cooped up in the cabin of a ship while on the roll.

Latitude 32° 34' S., longitude 9° 34' W., which indicates that the *Ganges* is again on her good behaviour. Temperature, 67F.

21 August – We have now got into it; the waves began to look respectable, as they heaved upwards and then curled their monstrous tops, and came down in a torrent of foam. At last we had passed the latitude of Cape Town, having reached about a degree farther south.

Twelve o'clock noon today found us tearing through a heavy sea at 11 knots. I heard my boy crying out as he viewed the billows, 'There they come, hill over hill – hold fast.'

At five o'clock a loud crack like a shot was heard to resound through the ship. The main-top studding sail had split. Another was immediately brought to replace it, so anxious was the captain to take the full advantage of the favouring gale. It had been scarcely rigged out when, like its predecessor, it was ripped in two. After that premonition, we did not try a third.

A decent Scotchwoman (Mrs. McWatt), in the midships cabin, at half-past three today, chose to give birth to a boy. Alas, this was a rough sea for such an event; however, she was safely delivered by Mr. Welby, our surgeon; but about half an hour after the birth the child began to show unfavourable symptoms, and about half-past seven o'clock at night the little being breathed its last.

Had that domestic incident occurred in calmer and warmer latitudes, and mother and child gained some ten days headway, there might have been a good chance of the little one surviving; in this stormy, old region it was scarcely to be expected.

About ten o'clock at night a fierce squall suddenly struck the ship, and shivered a stunsail to ribbons. The bow of the *Ganges* appeared to shoot down like an arrow into the trough of the sea. All was bustle in taking in canvas, and rapidly executing the as rapid orders that were successively bellowed forth from the poop.

Latitude 34° 39' S., longitude 5° 33' W., which gave a long run since yesterday, with 201 miles of easting.

22 August – At one o'clock this morning another violent squall assailed us. It drew the ship through the water at 13 knots, which, at all events, was a satisfactory result, and, fortunately, we also came about two points up to the wind, which somewhat eased the ship. The squall abated, but it continued to blow hard throughout the night, and carried us cheerily onward on our south-east course.

At seven o'clock in the morning, after the day dawned, the Union Jack was brought out, and the remains of the little child were consigned to the deep.

It was very cold today and pilot-coats were in requisition, but the sun shone forth. At nine o'clock the thermometer stood at 62F in the cabin but when taken upon deck it sunk as low as 57F, which was a material difference from 80F to 84F, to which we were accustomed for a while.

The death which our ship had given to the never-ceasing records of mortality, I suspect must be left to the ship's log, for the Registrar-General in Scotland,[11] the recent domicile of the parents, would not gather any increase to his flock by the event.

I have been reminded by this episode of a little incident I once witnessed. It was so far back as 1836, when I was journeying from Edinburgh to Dumfries by the road, which leads through the romantic pass of Dalveen.[12]

Although in the beginning of May, the day was hard, with a biting, cold wind. As we passed through a moorland pastoral track, we saw a new-born lamb. The coachman exclaimed, when he heard the bleating of the newly born animal, 'Aye! Aye! mae, mae, lambie, ye have cam into a cauld world.' There was a sentiment in the observation which was characteristic of our countrymen. Had some English connoisseur thrown out his comment in passing, it would have probably run after this fashion, 'Ay! Ay! young un, I hope some day soon to pay my best respects to you, when I see you alongside a nice salad.'

Towards evening the wind, which had been astern, moderated, and came more upon our quarter. Accordingly, spanker, trysail, and staysails were set. The moon shone brightly forth, and it was fortunate that that luminary would be with us on the nights that we were rounding the Cape.

Latitude 36° 44' S., longitude 1° 10' W., which gave us a run of about 260 miles during the preceding 24 hours – not a bad day's work.

23 August – We have had a tumbling night of it – not much wind, but a swell so heavy that, the officer of the middle watch remarked on the antics of the ship.

It snatched sleep from many an eye; in fact our frigate had not experienced such throes during the voyage. Water cans and many other articles got on the loose and knocked about. In the forenoon the sea had fallen, and the wind blew lightly on the port-quarter. There were occasional glimpses of sunshine, but the atmosphere was rather hazy.

When the deck service was commenced today, I wished I had some clever artist, to have portrayed the expressive twinkle that came from the boatswain's little, bright, dark eye, as he stood with a rope in his hand (for he is never idle).

He has been on former voyages with Captain Funnell, who tells me that he is a fine sailor, which I can well believe. He is the father of nine children. Their Dad is now far, far at sea, but, no doubt, with the hope of returning within twelve months.

After tea we suddenly heard a jolly chorus arise on the quarter deck, and thinking it came from some of the steerage passengers, we deemed it strange conduct for a Sunday night. It turned out, however, that it came from the sailors, as they were pumping out the bilge water.

The chant commenced either in German or Dutch, for we have several foreigners among our crew. But our English tars must have their turn too, and so the ditty resolved into their vernacular. I heard something about, 'a nice young girl is Sally Brown', and also, 'I wish I was in Liverpool', which was sung right lustily.

At night we were going at 11 knots, with a fine stiff wind, and the ship was more steady than she had been for the last few days. We have at last passed over the meridian of Greenwich, and our time was nearly the same as at Lowestoft, on the coast of Suffolk, which, I believe, is the easternmost limit of Great Britain. We considered ourselves now round the corner, or past the Rubicon, and well on with our voyage; but we have many a mile of easting yet before us, and there was nothing like good strong winds for urging us onward.

Latitude 38° 11' S., longitude 2° 0' E. The temperature was 58F in the forenoon.

24 August – The night had been what we may reckon quiet, after the toss we had on the preceding evening. We reached 11 knots, but it was thought prudent to take in stunsails and royals, as it looked rather squally. The morning felt chilly, and resembled a bright October day in Scotland. In the cabin the thermometer stood at 60F at 12 o'clock noon, but, of course, it would have been a few degrees colder outside.

Last night, a young gentleman, or rather lad, one of the cabin passengers, fell as he was coming down the poop stair, and came in contact with the binnacle, the glass of which was broken, and the compass driven away. He was a good deal shaken, but was soon back on his feet.

Towards the afternoon the wind died away, and we in consequence rolled heavily at the mercy of the swell, forcing us to be wary at dinner, for the soup and other liquids became very restless; but we have become accustomed to that rolling, and take it very coolly, although we occasionally, when off our guard, come bump against the bulkheads.

I discovered that I was black and blue in more than one place, but know not when and where the knocks were received, so little are those matters heeded amongst us.

Latitude 39° 14' S., longitude 7° 4' E. Temperature 60F in the cabin.

25 August – We have had a good deal of rain during the morning, with little wind. The sun faintly appeared, and it was comparatively warm. Someone remarked to the captain, as he was seated beside me, 'This was a fine day,' to which our chief responded that he considered it 'a very nasty one'. 'Tis the strong wind which blows and drives us onward that our officers hold to be good weather.

The tropical weather at sea was very trying to all sorts of machinery, so much rust gathered about the iron. Recourse was had to the carpenter or Old Chips, as he is termed, a skilful and invaluable man on board our ship, and in receipt of £7 a month. He was a tall, stout Prussian, and a quiet, good natured man.

The top was removed and part of the machinery taken down, when vinegar and then oil were applied to eat away the rust and lubricate the parts. In these operations Chips was ably seconded by a respectable man named Hudson; a blacksmith from Pollokshaws. The latter had an anvil and bellows among his effects, and was going to set up in business as soon as he landed in Auckland.

In the evening a breeze came slightly abaft our beam, and we soon made 7 to 8 knots. At ten o'clock the log indicated 10½ knots, and the ship at the same time went very steadily. Our position was latitude 39° 24' S., longitude 9° 0' E. Within the last 24 hours we had, therefore, only made 10 miles of southing and 88 of easting.

Mr. Woolley, our first officer, who took charge of the log book, should have a better tale to tell tomorrow. We have now reached a parallel south of Melbourne and Sydney, being about on the same latitude as the Bass Straits, which separated Tasmania or, as it was formerly named Van Diemen's Land, from Australia. We were also several degrees south of our destination, Auckland, which lies 166 degrees of longitude east from the point we made today.

26 August – There had been a fine wind during the night. It happily continued abaft the beam, so that every sail which was set filled, and carried us along at from 11 to 12 knots. This speed kept up today, and the motion was delightfully smooth. The weather was fine, the thermometer standing at 62F in the cabin, and the sun began to break forth at 12 noon which would allow an observation.

At that moment the passengers forward were engaged in a raffle for a revolver. The dice were thrown on the face of the capstan. As Marryat somewhere tritely observed, 'In cold weather people like to congregate round the fire.' We have no fire, and do not require it; but as the nights were now cold, there was less promenading of the deck, and ladies and gentlemen found it very snug to gather in the saloon, where there was no lack of amusement.

Still, reading was the grand and permanent resource; and that reminded me of what Lord Jeffrey[13] said in one of his letters, which I trust I may be pardoned in quoting, as the thoughts were so true and so beautifully expressed, especially as we do feel their force at sea.

'If I were to pray for a taste which should stand me in stead, and be a source of happiness and cheerfulness to one throughout life, and a shield against its ills, it would be a taste for reading.'

A little before the 'gloamin' I walked along to the forecastle to see how things were getting on. How pleasant it was to look up into the rigging and see every sail drawing its full bellyful of wind, and the *Ganges* was exceeding 12 knots.

After ten o'clock in the evening, when the private lights must all be doused, according to the rules of the ship, I had a few minutes pleasant conversation with the captain, who, poor man, had not left the deck since five o'clock in the morning, with the exception of the short period devoted to breakfast, dinner, and tea, so anxiously alive was he to his duty.

He was proposing to turn in for an hour, and to go on deck again at 12 midnight, when the middle watch was set. I suspect he will have but fitful rest, as he was suspicious about the night.

Latitude 39° 33' S., longitude 14° 44' E. That gives nine miles of southing, but nearly 5 degrees of easting, and the latter may be computed at about 274 miles. That is fine sailing, especially when it is taken into account that nearly six of the 24 hours elapsed yesterday before the sails commenced to fill.

27 August – The prognostications of our captain proved only too correct, although the enemy appeared earlier than he had anticipated. It was about half past twelve midnight when a furious gale came out of the northward, or off the coast of Africa, and on to our stern. The second officer, who was on the watch, was driven from the after to the forward part of the poop before its force, and the ship rushed through the water at upwards of 11 knots.

All hands were immediately piped, and set to take in and save the sails, which would soon have gone to ribbons. The ship gave two or three violent, convulsive rolls, heavier than any we have yet experienced.

This roused most of the passengers, male and female. The men came on deck, and it was as well they did, for there are some brawny arms among them, which were soon brought into play and assisted the sailors to pull the ropes.

This extra aid was very timeous and welcome, as it enabled the urgent operations to be executed with greater celerity, for it must be remembered that a merchant vessel, however well manned, is not like a man-of-war, where every brace has its appointed hands, and every mast from top to deck, its chosen crew.

Her Majesty's service had, accordingly, less excuse than our mercantile navy for the loss of sails on emergency. As it was, the *Ganges* was at length shorn of her canvas and left scudding before the wind, with nothing set except three topsails, closely reefed, and her foresail, or well nigh under bare poles, being an aspect she had not until now exhibited. It continued to blow hard throughout the night, but the sea was not so high as it would have been had the wind not been off the land.

In the hurry and confusion they had omitted to call up Old Chips. He, honest fellow, having faced many a south-wester and north-easter in his day, lay asleep in his berth, as I did myself, and also my boy, no way disturbed by the noise and fearful heaving of the ship, as it had been described to me by our mariners.

He was, however, very grumpy in the morning, on discovering the work that had been carried out, and he had not been among the labouring crew. In his German-English, he said, 'By Got, for the many years he'd been on the sea, he'd never been used so demmd badly.'

As for Old Pipes, the boatswain, although, of course, like the carpenter, sailmaker, and cook, he is not included in the regular watch, he was not long in being at his post after the alarm was sounded, as the sailors, especially the apprentices, knew to their cost, for his gruff voice pierced to the lowest depth of his acoustic organs.

This morning, when I awoke at six o'clock, I soon saw that something had been up, for, although on going to bed I left, as I thought, the various articles in my cabin quietly interned, I soon spotted that they had burst free during the night, and presented a woeful scene of wreck and confusion.

The coverlet had gone by the board, the floor was strewed with clothing, the contents had escaped from certain of the pockets, and, worse than all, a snuff box, with a quaint device on the lid, being a parting token from a good and faithful friend in Glasgow, had got completely shattered. My own straw hat and that of my boy had come down from aloft, the latter most artistically capping the former. Amidst it all, I slept as comfortably as if I had been in my old domicile in St. George's Road, opposite to the mansion of a highly respected ex-Lord Provost of Glasgow.[14]

Our young men in the cabin were not behind during the night in their readiness to bear a hand. The captain jocularly remarked to them at breakfast that they had been the means of saving the sails, a verdict which I scarcely think our friend Pipes would have readily endorsed.

I only mention that when the word is passed to pipe all hands, the appointed duty of the carpenter was to stand by the main tack, and the sailmaker follows suit, while the cook goes forward to let go the foresheet.

Last night our young purser, Mr. Spencer Sutton, was called up, and was soon on duty at the foretop, for he is also a seaman, having passed the statutory examination, and acted as an officer on more than one voyage along with our present captain, who was then also an officer.

In the forenoon there was a good deal to do in unfurling and setting sail, and all were lending their aid, including several of the passengers. When the sailors were busily engaged forward, I saw our captain on the poop stoutly hauling at the main topgallant brace.

One of our young friends, Mr. Nalder, a fine youth from Somersetshire, and every inch a man, had hold next to the captain, and my little fellow took the succeeding turn; from them the rope was sent to the poop gangway below, where the first officer and boatswain passed with their best violence.

Two men were now at the wheel, and there may be more before we are through with it. She does rock in fine style; but, as the captain cheerily says, 'Never mind, we are going on our course rejoicing.' At five o'clock in the afternoon, it blew strongly, with occasional squalls. One of our studding sail booms snapped, and we had to be wary of the sail we carried.

On the foremast there were the foresails and upper and lower topsails; on the main the two topsails and topgallant; and on the mizzen, only the lower topsail.

This day (Thursday the 27th) happens to be the birthday of Mr. Thomas Sutton, an elder brother of our purser, and a universal favourite, so much has he contributed to enliven our ocean pilgrimage. He is still in the prime of manhood, belongs to Maidstone, the county town of Kent, and years since succeeded his late respected father in the management of a large building business, including many contracts for important public works.

In the midst of an active career declining health came, and his friends, who were many and true hearted, advised a temporary surcease from toil, along with a change of clime. He therefore had availed himself of the opportunity of sailing in the same ship with his younger brother.

It would require a Dickens to sketch him. His humour was of an eccentric cast; he could go off on a tangent and there was always a method in what he said – nothing meaningless or vacant in his observations, which were set off with a fine voice, a handsome countenance, and a most expressive dark eye. Woe to any person who rashly attempted to vulgarly chaff him. In such an encounter the assailant generally came off second best, as so remarkable was his fluency and command of the English language.

Withal, he was a kind-hearted, highly honourable man, and gifted with shrewd business talents. May he be happy and prosperous where he is going, is the warm and generous wish of all his fellow passengers. Of course, we had a little quiet festivity on the occasion, and all passed off happily, notwithstanding the weather which was rather uncouth, and a leg of mutton bolted from the table into the lap of Mr. Green, whose birthday we celebrated on the 4th of the month, a few weeks past.

Latitude 39° 43' S., longitude 20° 44' E. We have now, therefore, got to the east of the Cape of Good Hope, and have made rapid way under the influence of those strong winds. Temperature, about 61 F.

28 August – We have had a stormy night, with much rolling, which aroused not a few out of their slumbers, and made them vacate their berths. A barrel broke loose among the stores below the cuddy, and smashed several hundred bottles which were luckily empty.

It was a bleak, stormy day, with heavy falls of rain, and a raw, piercing wind. The wind was still astern, and consequently we rolled heavily.

At six o'clock at night the weather brightened, and we went along with stunsails and royals, at nine knots, which drew to upwards of ten knots when the ten o'clock, or four bells, log was hove. The moon shone out brightly, and it was such a beautiful sight that I did not care to turn in until 12 o'clock midnight – an example which one or two of my young friends followed.

Latitude 39° 24' S., longitude 26° 1' E., which gave us an excellent run – and all the better that we had gained a few miles to the northward, for we had no wish for the present to go farther south if we could help it. Last night, there was a special service, or thanksgiving, in the midships cabin, among the steerage passengers, for the safety of the ship during the last few rather stormy days.

Temperature, about 60F in the cabin.

29 August – The wind continued too much astern, but still we had been going through the night at ten knots, and matters have been comparatively quiet.

It was a beautiful morning; indeed, when I looked out early and felt the air, I thought of Byron's description of the night waning, the vapours round the mountains curling and melting into morning as light awoke the world. Really, today there was health in the gale and freshness in the stream.

Still, the *Ganges* was in a saucy humour, and was now rolling most jollily, as the wind had fallen and given her too much of her own way. It was of no use to attempt to hold on by a desk and write in a decorous, sober fashion like, for example, the talented and respected minister of the Cumbrae Isles, sitting in his picturesque manse, and no doubt at present preparing a homily to be listened to by some of my esteemed friends tomorrow. And destined also to illumine a few natives of Glasgow, situated on 'the adjacent Isle of Great Britain',[15] who repair there on the Saturday night to gulp their weekly mouthfuls of air.

Little did I think, this day last year, as I was sojourning on that green island, that I would be tossing about here (very comfortably, however) today. Alas! we little know what is before us; and perhaps the less the better, as my humorous friend Tom Sutton suddenly came out with yesterday – 'If my poor mother had lived to see that her dear Thomas was to be out here, she'd have been in a regular fret about me! Wouldn't she?' I thought other and dear departed mothers besides his would have also had their own thoughts about them who are now far away.

The wind at two o'clock in the afternoon came more upon our port quarter, and we got nine knots. Still, our good lady rolled most unmannerly for when I came out of my cabin to sit down to dinner, the first prospect that greeted me was the soup plentifully oozing out of the tureen on to the tablecloth.

We spotted a vessel ahead, and thought that we would come up with her at ten o'clock in the evening; but so superior were our sailing powers that we came abreast of her a little after eight and blazed a light to indicate our vicinage. The stranger made no counter-sign, probably judging that silence was the wisest policy; for, supposing this was some Australian trader, she would deem it better that the world should be ignorant of the knowledge that she was thus outstripped.

At 11 o'clock in the evening the wind came still farther on the port quarter and we careered along at 12 knots. I produced a solitary bottle of Campbeltown whisky, which I have carried all this length. I treated some of my chosen friends, including two of the officers, and of course Tom Sutton. Its fine quality soon sealed its doom, for it was universally pronounced too good to live.

Latitude 39° 19' S., longitude 30° 35' E., the ship having run about 244 miles. Temperature 59F. The day is stretching out as we get east. It will be light until about seven o'clock when we reach the longitude of Auckland.

30 August – A beautiful Sunday morning. The wind had veered to our starboard quarter, and the fore studsails were set both on the weather and lee-side. The *Ganges* stalked the waves in trim array, like some fair virgin on her bridal day. Shortly after 11 o'clock in the morning, the wind blew more strongly, and the sea rose.

I was standing on deck sedately conversing with Mr. Willan, the Yorkshire farmer, who was descanting to me on the merits of a brown collie dog of the gentler sex, which had unfortunately died in the course of the night – 'She was joost two ye'r ould, and aboot cooming to her prime' – when our colloquy was cut short by the ship suddenly giving a violent lurch, which set him and me, along with a pretty little boy, off balance.

We were only brought up, or rather brought down, when we struck against the spare spars, and found ourselves stretched on the deck with our feet in the lee scuppers. My bucolic friend got off easily, as his lower limbs were encased in tight leather leggings; but I received a blow on the cheekbone, a slight cut on the hand, and a smart smash on the shins. We, however, soon gathered ourselves up, and proceeded to lift the boy, who was crying piteously, having received a severe stroke on the knee.

Soon afterwards six persons, including a tall lady and her husband, all went down at the same place, and my fair friend unfortunately caught an additional black eye, for

A painting by E. Noyce c.1852–1860. The scene shows the last moments of emigrants on their native soil before boarding a vessel bound for the southern hemisphere. A combination of busy preparation for departure and sadness at leaving friends and relatives – most of whom they would never see again – and a situation remarked upon by Buchanan as the Ganges *prepared for sail from Gravesend. Courtesy of the Alexander Turnbull Library, Wellington, New Zealand*

she was already gifted with a bright pair. The ship continued to roll furiously, but one gets used to it, as well as to the loud creaking of the timbers.

Latitude 39° 17' S., longitude 35° 26' E. Temperature 61½F. We cannot expect much variation in the temperature at present, as for the last seven days we have been sailing off and on the 39th parallel south.

31 August – A fine fair wind during the night, which gave 10 to 12 knots. The morning was rainy and gusty, with the wind too much astern. Most of the passengers were seeking the comfortable shelter of the cabin. Tom Sutton has been reading Professor Aytoun's[16] poem on the death of the gallant Montrose to the ladies, and which he has done with excellent emphasis.

At six o'clock at night we were going at 12 knots with only the square sails, including royals, set, but, as we were sitting down to tea, the wind, which had been on the port, suddenly veered to the starboard quarter, coming off from the north-westward in a violent squall. All was bustle on deck and in the rigging as the royals and mizzen topgallant were taken in. It was evident that we were going to have a boisterous night, but one comfort was that there was good moonlight.

At 11 o'clock in the evening I had three minutes talk with the captain as he came down to get out a pair of gloves, or rather mittens. As he stood in his oil-skins, with his fine weather-beaten, manly features shining out beneath his south-wester, looking under the light of the cabin lamp so serene and cheery at the thought of the way his ship would gain before the powerful gale, he would have made a fine subject for the pencil of an eminent limner.

He reminded me in some degree of the figure of the American officer who brought the British discovery ship *Resolution* across the Atlantic, as portrayed in a cartoon of *Punch*. This vessel was abandoned near to Melville Island, in 1853, and two years afterwards was found by an American whaler floating in Baffin's Bay, having drifted all that distance eastward through Barrow's Straits and Lancaster Sound, on the pack ice. The Government of President Buchanan of Canada, in a generous spirit, worthy of all admiration, paid the salvage money, refitted the vessel, and restored it to Queen Victoria.

Our captain, as he turned to go on deck, said to me – 'The ship would not require some snuff to make her sneeze tonight.' It did blow as I turned into my berth and lay down quite snug under the circumstances.

Latitude 39° 20' S., longitude 40° 16' E.

---

1. Aberdonian: a resident of Aberdeen in the north-east of Scotland. David Buchanan was born in and spent his early years in Montrose, which is to the south-east of the Howe of the Mearns, a rich farming area just south of the city of Aberdeen.

2. Buchanan's estimate here was in error by over 1000 miles.

3. The Ramshorn is a famous old Glasgow church which is located in what was the mercantile area of the city in the 18th century, and which nowadays is known as the Merchant City.

4. An 18th-century Glasgow merchant who owned plantations in the West Indies.

5. See July, note 7.

6. An observation that hints at the old Scottish Presbyterian belief, still rigorously preached during the 19th century, that one should not desecrate the Lord's day or sabbath with work of any kind, however trifling.

7. See July, note 17.

8. Gabions are cylinders filled with earth that were used for building fortifications, or in the construction of engineering works.

9. The Tontine Hotel was an old Glasgow landmark located in the city's Trongate at Glasgow Cross. It started life as a coffee house and meeting place for the city's old mercantile elite in the very late 18th century. It later became a popular recruiting spot for the nation's army regiments.

10. See July, note 5.

11. The Registrar General is the official in charge of the General Register Office of Scotland, the national registry in Edinburgh for the registration of births, deaths and marriages in Scotland.

12. The Pass of Dalveen is located about 25 miles to the north-east of the town of Dumfries in the Lowther Hills. Today it is reached by travelling along the A702 linking the villages of Durisdeer and Elvanfoot. Murray's handbook for Scotland, published in 1894, described it as a magnificent drive by carriage alongside the Powtrail Burn and through the Dalveen Pass. The country either side of the Pass is typical sheep-farming terrain.

13. Lord Francis Jeffrey, 1773–1850, was a Scottish judge and critic. He studied at Glasgow and Oxford and was the Lord Rector of Glasgow University in 1820 and 1832. After a spell as MP for Perth and then Edinburgh he was made a judge at the Court of Session. In 1802 he was a co-founder of the influential literary magazine *The Edinburgh Review*.

14. The Glasgow, and Scottish, equivalent of the English Lord Mayor of a town or city.

15. The islands of Great Cumbrae and Little Cumbrae lie in the Clyde estuary, about fifteen minutes' sail from the town of Largs on the coast of west Ayrshire. In the 19th century the local Church of Scotland minister, the Rev. James Adam, in his church in the Great Cumbrae island town of Millport always included a prayer in his service for the people of Great Cumbrae and the adjacent islands of Great Britain and Ireland.

16. William Edmonstoune Aytoun, 1813–65, was a Scottish poet and humorist. In 1845 he was appointed Professor of Rhetoric and Belles Lettres at Edinburgh University.

September 1863

1 September – The first day of the partridge shooting, as some of my young English friends, Mr. Green, Mr. Stopford, and Mr. Nalder did not require to be told; but no such sport for them out here, unless they were to let fly at the Cape pigeons, who could be killed by the dozen. But the use of firearms is very properly strictly prohibited, as a rolling ship is no place for smallarms, unless in the event of a pirate assailing us, of which there is no chance in those latitudes.

Even if such an improbable contingency did ensue, our situation would not be so hopeless. It is true that we would have no chance at long range, for we have only one six-pounder or signal gun aboard. Our strength would be close quarters, as we have not only a supply of round shot and canister for our said six-pounder, but an ample store of smallarms, including fowling pieces, rifles, and revolvers.

I know not how we stand as to side arms, but we could use marling spikes as boarding pieces, and we could also bring our butcher's cleavers into play. Above all, inclusive of the crew, we have at least 140 men, stout and true, who would not fail us in the hour of need.

Thus equipped, I think the *Ganges* may exclaim, as to the general run of piratical craft, in the words of Border chivalry – 'My name is Jock Elliot – wha daur meddle wi' me?'[1]

Anyone would think I was getting into a warlike mood this forenoon. Perhaps it is the strong, merry gale which still prevails (for more than once this MS has been driven into my lap) that has a tendency to stir the blood. I am of a pacific disposition; for, some years ago, after some self-denial, I declined to purchase a revolver, wishing to live at peace with all men.

At 12 midnight last night the wind became more wild, and all sail had to be taken in except the topsails and foresail, the former being closely reefed. The second officer, my countryman, Valentine, had his cap blown overboard, though it had seemed a tight fit.

During the height of the gale, the ship ran before it at nearly 15 knots, and the average rate throughout the night was upwards of 12. It was difficult to heave the log, owing to the heavy sea running on the stern having had a tendency to drive the float forward.

At four o'clock in the morning it commenced to pour down hail so fiercely that one might have gathered a snowball off the deck. That was rather a contrast to the weather we had experienced some weeks since, when we were in the same latitude as that of the great African desert.

In the morning, as I walked out on the deck, I found it comparatively quiet. Many passengers were fatigued having lost their rest during the night. However, one or two children were running about much the same as usual, for they keep their feet in all weathers, and when they fall they little heed, as they appear to be as hard as nails.

In particular, there is one little Yorkshire man named Jonas, the son of Mr. Willan, and only three or four years old, who may be seen cruising about in all seasons. He is like a round ball, but his father would be unlikely to bestride a horse that was surer footed than is merry little Jonas.

For the first time last night I closed my port, for it was cold and stormy. I, however, looked up on the deck at eight bells, or 12 o'clock, midnight and found a clear moonlight.

Latitude 39° 15' S., longitude 46° 15' E., the ship having made a run of upwards of 280 miles. At this rapid rate we would be at Auckland in 22 days. Temperature at night in cabin was as low as 52F.

2 September – We may exclaim this morning that the air bites shrewdly; and no wonder, for the thermometer on the deck went down to 42F, and the water was quite cold. This is rather a transition for those who were lately for weeks in a temperature ranging from 80F to 84F; but we must take what the gods provide for us, and be thankful for as much.

In the morning I had partially opened my port, when I soon saw the hail rattling over my coverlet. It was the prelude to three or four violent lurches, which dashed my water can loose and flooded the floor of my cabin. We continued to have glimpses of sunshine, varied by heavy hail showers, and they have been snow-balling each other on the main deck.

The ship, however, goes at a great rate under her topsails and foresail, to which have been added the main and fore-topgallant sails, along with the main trysail. During the seven days terminating last Sunday at noon, we had accomplished 1,544 miles, which is precious good work for any ship. I remember, in the days of the Leith smacks,[2] seven days used to be considered not a long passage between Leith and London. It had been made in three days, but that was very exceptional, as it is a rather trying voyage, demanding both westing and easting.

A rather near and dear relative of my own was once seventeen days between Aberdeen and London. But in these times there was some chance of adventure on a coasting voyage on the German Ocean.[3] On that last occasion, the captain, a quiet, staid Aberdonian, was seen to turn quite fierce, when he drew forth the powder, wadding, and shot, as he was preparing to make resistance to a vessel which in the distance they suspected to be a French privateer.

They were alas boarded by the navy's press gang – a most odious institution to honest seafaring men. There was only one man liable to impressment, a stout, brawny seaman. They were at a loss at first of how to conceal him. At last they thought of an expedient, which was to place him at the foot of my friend's berth, below the bed clothes, she taking her place on the top.

As he was stopping in, his eye caught his coarse shoes lying on the cabin floor, and, of course, these evidences were immediately stowed away. In this state, the lieutenant in command of the press gang boat's crew came down to the cabin, and was told by the captain (pointing to the berth) that there was only a sick lady there – a fib which his guardian angel would surely blot out.

The navy officer was quite satisfied, took his glass of grog with great complacency, and made his exit. When the poor fellow came forth, he shook himself and bolted out of the cabin, for he became the mark of the surrounding jests on the rather peculiar position he had occupied in reference to the fair young lady, for such she most truly was. She said that while she was undergoing this penance she could distinctly mark the heavy throbbing of the powerful chest of him who lay below in an agony of anxiety, and bathed in perspiration.

Talking of those Leith smacks, they were fine vessels of their class. When a boy, and living not far from what now forms the Parliamentary boundary between Edinburgh and Leith, the favourite pastime of our gang was to repair to Leith Harbour and Docks on Saturday, and many more of our High School holidays.

There we would get a boat, and pull about; but we grew discontented with the limits of the harbour, and would have a row out to seaward. Then we wanted to have canvas as well as oars, but fortunately for us we could not acquire the latter type of craft.

We knew every London smack, the *Czar, Hawk, Delight, Pilot, Trusty, Superb, Ocean, Earl of Wemyss, Sir Walter Scott*, &c. The whalers – the *Dexterity, William* and *Ann*, etc., the last-named being an old French man-of-war which had been captured – were household words amongst us.

Nay, we went further, for we were intimate with some of the West Indian traders, especially the *Isabella Simpson*, the principal cabin of which we were once privileged to examine. The object which especially attracted our youthful eyes was the mizzen mast – which of course passed through the deck in this quarter of the ship – encircled with a stand of smallarms. Of all things, firearms are the envy of boys, and the fortunate possessor of a pistol is even more highly courted than the owner of a watch.

These London smacks carried a huge mainsail, requiring at least eight men for the hoist, which enabled them to go very near the wind. They were also very safe vessels, for I only recollect of two being driven ashore – the *Earl of Wemyss* in 1833, and, if my memory serves me, the *Delight* at another period – no lives lost in either case.

The one named in honour of Sir Walter Scott was, like the rest, finally converted into a clipper or schooner for the goods trade; when the steamers rendered the passenger traffic not worth an old song, indifferently honest recruits, *en route* to Chatham, and wholly dishonest convicts on their way to the hulks, became the primary articles of live export by the once famous London and Leith smacks.

Sir Walter Scott, in testimony of the honour rendered to him, made a present of colours to the smack that bore his name. But our great man of the North had not acted with his usual circumspection, for he chose the Royal Navy bunting instead of the white border Union Jack, which is distinctive of the mercantile navy. The consequence was that the *Sir Walter Scott*, on her first voyage, was brought to by a gun fired across her bows – was boarded, overhauled, and never more dared to show that flag. It was returned to Sir Walter Scott, and used to be hoisted periodically at his residence in Abbotsford.

But I was forgetting that I was aboard the *Ganges*, crossing the Indian Ocean, and 2,350 miles south of the line. As Goldsmith[4] said in his *Traveller* (and I quote from memory) –

'Where'er I roam, whatever realms I see,

My heart, untravelled, fondly turns to thee.'

I need not forget that I am at sea, for, as the surgeon at present remarked to me and Mr. Woolley, the first officer, who sat beside me writing up his log, 'There is a strong chain of coincidence aboard ship.' Outside the wind was howling through the rigging at that exact moment, and smash went some crockery, mingled with knives and forks. The spray was flying over the forecastle, as a torrent of foam, which would have blanketed Glasgow's George Square, rolled out from the bows. Then I dared not let go the hold of an ink bottle, a book, or any article, or else I would have to go in quest of it and probably not find it improved by its escapade.

To crown it all, a party of ladies along with, I am ashamed to say, only one gentleman, who presided at the concertina, were practising the music for the Sunday service. The first officer gave me quaint looks as the tune went off key, and he continued to work on the longitude of the day.

The wind in the afternoon was not so favourable, being too much over the starboard bow. The captain was not pleased with the steering, having to take in canvas when he thought there was no occasion for it, had there been skilful steering; he accordingly got hold of the wheel himself, and showed how sails were won, or, more literally speaking, the wind taken at its utmost vantage.

While at dinner today, my thoughts strayed from my plate, which contained excellent pease soup, and the contents were suddenly discharged into my lap. All the sympathy for my mishap was a peal of laughter, in which my friend the captain loudly joined, and which was re-echoed by those who were seated below the mizzen mast when they found out what had occurred.

Latitude 39° 10' S., longitude 51° 35' E.

3 September – The weather, as we may expect, with the wind blowing from the cold south, was still chill and blustering. Few ventured out of doors yesterday, and I have not seen many of the forward passengers for a day or two. Our ladies, however, behave very gallantly, for they borrow our sea coats, and gird a strap round. Thus accoutred, they mount the poop or quarter deck, which I need scarcely say is reserved for the cabin passengers exclusively.

During the night we had a strong wind, and were going along in the right course at 10½ knots, which was good sailing, seeing that we were not enabled to carry much canvas. Nothing was set except the three courses, three tops, and the main and fore skysail jibs.

As I was sitting alone in the cuddy last night, about half-past 11 o'clock, reading by the light of the solitary lamp, the youngest apprentice came in to see the clock before sounding the seven bells of the evening watch. He is an interesting-looking, intelligent youth, belonging to Liverpool, and this was his first voyage, he being indentured for four years. He was making rapid progress in distinguishing the various braces and halyards; and as the boatswain said to me one day, when I was inquiring after the youth, and if he was getting on well, 'Ay, ay, sir, he's too clever for me!'

Another, but a very different person from worthy Pipes, viz., a good and pious matronly lady, told me that she had conversed with the boy, who had said to her that he did not like the sea and intended to quit it for good and all on his return to England. She seemed to think that the resolve was very natural, if not laudable. I deemed otherwise, but said nothing.

A few days afterwards my boy told me that Edward Lowe, for that is his name, was anxious for a book to read, and he asked my permission to lend him a copy of *Robinson Crusoe*, as Edward had a chest and would take care of the volume. Of course, I gladly consented. He always smiles when I meet him; but last night, when he came into the cabin, he seemed to wish to talk with me, and the conversation resolved into his own future.

I advised him to continue to improve in the practical part of a seaman's duty, and to read in his spare time – above all, to attend to writing and arithmetic. If he did so – looked to his calling as, at least, his chief worldly care, was sober, and conducted himself well, I said that I saw no reason why he might not in time acquire navigation, and one day be the commander of a ship like that in which he now occupied the junior station.

'Especially (I added) give up all thoughts of leaving the sea – seeing you have already made it your occupation – for if you go home in that mind, people will think you fickle or unsteady; and you may be sent to become a tailor, watchmaker, or some such quiet honest craft, with the knowledge that you have already shown yourself as an unenthusiastic sailor.'

He listened attentively, gratefully smiled, and said, 'Thank you kindly, sir.' I thought it a pity so nice a boy should be spoiled from becoming a seaman and a man; and so I hope Edward left me in a more resolute humour.

I also had a conversation with our second cook who was very bad with his hand, which has never recovered from a bite it received from that mad dog, the Irish cook's mate, on the night of the brawl, when the latter was put in irons.

As the day advanced we clapped on more sail. At two o'clock in the afternoon, when I took a survey of the rigging, I observed that we were carrying the outer and inner jibs, foretopmast staysail, the foresail, two tops, and topgallant; on the mainmast, the mainsail, two tops, topgallant, and royals; on the mizzen the cross-jack, the two tops, and topgallant.

The evening became comparatively quiet, the wind tending too much ahead, which took us off our course, and more to the northward than we were inclined; however, the farther north the warmer, so that it was an ill wind that does not bring something on the credit side.

Latitude 38° 47' S., longitude 56° 36' E. Temperature, about 53F.

4 September – This was a fine autumnal day, and the passengers began once more to come forth, like bees out of their hives, and walk in the sun, so far as the rolling swell will permit them.

The wind was favourable, but unfortunately too little of it, for we can only make six knots, although we have every square sail set. As yet we may be said to have escaped anything that may be termed really and seriously a storm.

What we have encountered was only what might have been reasonably expected. I have been out in more stormy weather in the German Ocean than I have experienced either in the North or South Atlantic, though its waves – and fierce enough they were too – might not have presented such a long, lofty, majestic roll.

I recollect especially coming through St. Andrews Bay – the Biscay Bay of the east coast of Scotland[5] – one day in a fine steamer called the *Britannia*, and which now runs on the Leith and Newcastle line, if not already purchased to run the American blockade.[6]

The wind literally roared as it passed through the rigging; the captain was an intimate friend of my own, and who has since received the thanks of the Governor of Victoria, along with a gold medal in testimony of his gallant conduct in rescuing the sufferers from the wreck of the *Admella*,[7] on the Australian coast.

On that day he never quitted the hurricane deck until we got under the lee of the Fife coast, as we fetched the mouth of the Firth of Forth. As for the mate, a knowing, cautious old salt, he stood by to direct the man at the wheel. The saloon table did not merely break loose from its moorings and tumble to the lee side with as much decorum as possible, but it performed a regular somersault, and stood with its heels in the air.

There was on board a friend of my own, a quiet Forfarshire laird, who has now found his resting place. He came to me on deck looking pale and shaky, saying, 'That is a terrible sea; is there any danger?' I saw his condition with half an eye, and chancing to have a flask in my pocket – in plain Scotch terms – administered to him 'a hearty dram'. He soon afterwards came up to me in a more composed state and said, 'Aye, that was very fine stuff you gave me; I think the sea is now rather fallen!'

I thought there would be some anxiety at home with one (now, unhappily for me, no more)[8] awaiting my return; on the contrary she gave a look of surprise on seeing me pop in, saying that she had been perfectly easy throughout the day, as she had concluded the vessel would never attempt the passage, or, at least, that I would not commit myself to it, in such a day of storm.

Today, out here in the Indian Ocean, the scene was quite serene. As I look out at the moment through the forward saloon door, I saw an active, comely matron, from the neighbourhood of Peterhead,[9] who had a tub placed beside the spare spars, and was chatting and washing away with as much composure as if she were on the banks of her own native stream, enjoying the delightful waters of the Youghie,[10] or in latitude 57° 30' N., longitude 1° 47' W., instead of being in latitude 38° 39' S., longitude 59° 38' E., as she was this day at noon.

I have been out in the German Ocean from 80 to 100 times – I had been across the English Channel, where there is often a tempestuous, short, angry sea, and more perilous to the mariner than the wide Atlantic or the Pacific – before I had that tussle in the *Ganges* on the second night of our present voyage.

These were coasting trips, the diameter of their orbit not exceeding some 600 miles; but still that cruise through St. Andrews Bay I deemed a more regular teaser than any I have encountered as yet in traversing several thousand miles of ocean.

It was now near that grateful epoch, the tea. In three hours hence, or at two bells (nine o'clock in the evening), comes the witching hour when the ladies and gentlemen all seem so kindly disposed to each other, and to all the world outside, the only active denizens of which now within our range of vision being the Cape pigeons, one of which was captured this afternoon.

I heard Mr. Woolley, who was at that moment poring over his chart, say that we were past the Mauritius. I used the freedom of coming athwart his survey, by asking him if that sweet voice, nigh the saloon door, did emanate from an Irish lady, who, with her husband and three pretty little cherubs, was now accompanying us.

Mr. Woolley, looking round, said I had guessed aright. 'Well,' I said, 'Woolley, I would not care much for the safety of our ship in a squall, if you were on the watch and gifted with a voice like that.' He laughed, and nodded acquiescence.

It is surprising to hear what loud deep tones issued from the little trunk of that firmly-built young sailor; the sound went from the poop to the forecastle, and reverberated through the ship as he thundered forth his mandates to 'heave the log', or 'pull the foretopgallant lee brace'; and what a bellow he could sing out.

5 September – We have had a quiet night; too quiet by far for our purposes. This morning the temperature is 58F, which we begin to think agreeable. We are now getting more acclimated to the cold, as we previously did to the heat.

The Cape pigeons are becoming too familiar for their own safety. I saw two albatross squat down in the midst of them, as conscious apparently of their own importance amidst the surrounding small fry. How gracefully those birds sit on the water!

Last night at tea the captain was telling us of the misfortunes while attending a vessel whose captain he knew, on her voyage from Calcutta to Bristol. A heavy sea struck her forward, swept away the boats, the cuddy, everything on deck in short, and, worse than all, the whole of the watch except the captain, who managed to lay hold of a rope, and afterwards swung himself down through the cabin skylight (or what remained of it) to save his wife, who was below along with another lady, the latter being their only passenger.

The captain succeeded in saving both of the females, but the cabin was a wreck, and completely gutted of everything, including all the female apparel. In this plight the poor lady passenger was compelled to adopt the maxim of duty before decoracy, and strut about wearing a coat and a pair of old continuations,[11] which had been kindly supplied to her from the wardrobe of the second mate. It was only when the ship touched at Madeira that she was able to doff her male attire.

A breeze sprung up at about 11 o'clock this forenoon, but, notwithstanding a pile of sail on every mast, we could not take more than six knots out of it.

My little fellow came down to me in the afternoon, quite cock-a-hoop, with a Cape pigeon in his hand, which he had hooked, being the fifth which has been caught. I paid the promised ransom, and offered him, I daresay with all safety to my pocket, half a crown if he could capture an albatross.

Encouraged by his success, he is again intent with his long line. He has got a holiday, this being Saturday, for we must not omit the time-honoured immemorial institutions of our native strand, and desecrate our Saturdays.

Later in the afternoon he caught another Cape pigeon which he gallantly presented to a young lady, having promised her the first fruits of his further success. She is to have it stuffed for posterity.

I heard just about five o'clock in the afternoon a loud shout on the main deck, and a steward told me that it was caused by a Cape pigeon. The captors had been meditating as to its fate, when the strong winged bird took the decision into its own talons, and darted out of their hands to rejoin its fellows. It is to be hoped that, having burst its bonds, it will not again be caught and brought back, with a lucky escape thus standing recorded against it.

Toward night the breeze freshened, and at nine o'clock we were going smoothly along, making 10½ knots, with the wind on our port beam.

Latitude 38° 29' S., longitude 60° 9' E.

6 September, Sunday – The fine wind on the port beam still favoured us. In the morning the speed was 12 knots, and at 12 o'clock noon it was 11 knots. The day was quiet, with an occasional gleam of sunshine. As for the temperature, we found it pleasant and bracing, but rather cold when the wind blew from the south.

The passengers have also had their appetite sharpened as compared with the period when they were passing through the tropics. The scale of the diet for the non-cabin passengers combined as much variety as the circumstances will permit.

On Monday it was boiled salt beef, rice and baked bread; on Tuesday, pease soup and pork; on Wednesday, preserved meat, soup and boulli; on Thursday, boiled beef and baked pies; on Friday, boiled beef and rice; on Saturday, pease soup and pork; and on Sunday, preserved beef, potatoes and dough.

I suppose there scarcely ever was a ship containing a large number of emigrants in which there were not occasional complaints, generally proceeding from some more difficult to please than others as to the quality of the portions of the provisions served out. This vessel is no exception.

I one day saw a man, but not a Scotsman, pitch his piece of pork overboard on receiving it, alleging that it was either too fat or too lean, I do not remember which; but, generally speaking, I think they were well pleased with the feed, and the arrangements made for their comfort. A good deal often depended upon themselves and their own forethought and aptitude for cookery.

The English passengers in this last respect decidedly excel the Scotch and the Irish, for the first named are more difficult to please. And that reminded me of an English artisan who had come to Montrose – a place famous for the excellence of its fish – but the culinary art was so deficient in this Englishman's estimation that one day he indignantly exclaimed, as he was sitting down to dinner, 'God sends the fish, but the devil sends the cooks!'

As for the cabin table, it is remarkably well supplied; for example, today we had cold salmon, roast ducks and green pease, being about the last of those feathered bipeds, roast mutton, roast pork, cold boiled pork, potatoes and rice – a supply of the latter cereal being invariably served up at breakfast and dinner. Then there were rhubarb and gooseberry tarts, and, lastly, a dessert – this only being served out on Sunday and Thursday.

The breakfast is also always varied and substantial. So I think it can be agreed that our creature comforts are by no means neglected on board the good ship *Ganges*.

The water in this temperate latitude, as it does taste to me, has become almost as fine and refreshing as Glasgow's supply from Loch Katrine.

In the afternoon, about five o'clock, it started to blow strongly. As I was standing on the main deck, gazing aloft at the rigging, and thinking what a beautiful fabric is a ship, whether majestically at rest on the unruffled calm of the waters, or flying gracefully along before the wind, as we were then doing, suddenly a belay pin broke, and freely went the foretopmast staysail with a noise that startled those who did not know what had occurred. As usual, on such like occasions, whether on sea or on shore, a crowd gathered near the scene, and were in the way of the sailors as they proceeded to recover and furl the rebellious sheet.

They little knew their danger, or that the block attached to the sheet had got loose, and would have brained any of the gaping throng had their heads chanced to come in its way. There is little sympathy for people if they heedlessly throw themselves in the way of danger.

As that magnanimous monarch, great statesman, and warrior, William of Orange, laconically and justly observed, when he was told that Bishop Walker had been killed at the battle of the Boyne, 'What business had he there?'

At night our speed was upwards of 11 knots.

Latitude 39° 20' S., longitude 65° 30' E.

7 September – A splendid breeze today – no sunshine, but a little rain. We kept at no less than 14 knots and upwards during the night, and are still at that speed. The *Ganges* was on her mettle, excelling at her work, and in too serious a mood to give way to those constant lurches, in which she was given to indulge in her lighter moments.

The captain, officers, and crew were all decked out in their storm coverings, and as the sea had risen, with a sharp roll now and then, there have been some mishaps on deck.

Some of our sailors, under the direction of the captain and purser, are actively engaged in trimming the ship, for our burden grows lighter as we get along. It cannot be otherwise, as upwards of 260 men, women, and children will cause a considerable hole in our breadbasket and store; and if nature abhors a vacuum, little is it coveted by a ship light in the water at most, as the *Ganges* has been since the outset of her present voyage.

Especially do we feel the effects caused by the displacement and emptying of the water casks. The alternative is to replenish with salt water, which we have been doing today in order to obtain sufficient ballast above the dead weight.

Today was the birthday of my second daughter,[12] and we have had, as is customary amongst us, a little festivity on the occasion. In the evening it was evident that, through the kindness of my good friend the purser, the baker had been instructed to exercise his best skill, for, in addition to our usual bountiful provisions, at tea we had fancy bread. A supply of sardines was also served up.

The night outside was gusty, dank, and dark, but 'the storm without might rair and rustle, Tam didna mind the storm a whistle'.[13] We were all very comfortable and pleasant.

Latitude 39° 40' S., longitude 72° 10' E., by dead reckoning. Temperature 62F in the morning, or warmer than we have experienced of late. Our run up to 12 o'clock today had been about 335 miles, or exceeding anything the ship had yet accomplished; indeed it would be good work even for the *Scotia* or *Persia* of the Cunard Line with its world wide reputation for speed, regularity, and safety.

8 September – The wind during the night, after changing direction, had nearly deserted us in the morning. It mattered not, for its favours were not worth receiving

Seven sketches from the illustrated New Zealand Herald c.1875, showing a number of scenes before and during an emigrants' voyage, most of which similar events and activities were described in Buchanan's journal. From the Making New Zealand Collection, courtesy of the Alexander Turnbull Library, Wellington, New Zealand

until it veered into our intended course. Had the strong breeze of yesterday remained constant to us, we should have been this forenoon past the small isle of St. Paul's,[14] situated in latitude 38° 47' S., longitude 77° 52' E. It is an important fishing station, but it was uninhabited, beyond a small settlement in connection with the fisheries.

The Cape pigeons, and also a greater number of albatrosses than I have as yet witnessed, were this morning hovering close to our wake. The lines were thrown out, as the water was calm. Mr. Nalder used a strong and a proper line for this big game. He was among the first to hook a Cape pigeon, and very few of these have been caught, notwithstanding the efforts of several of our young men.

At one o'clock in the afternoon a voice shouted down the aft cuddy confirming that an albatross was aboard. Instantly everyone was up on deck, where, sure enough, there was a beautiful bird, one of the finest of the feathered race, bleeding over the taffrail, for it was too violent a visitor to be kept alive, and handled with any freedom.

When hooked, it made a stern resistance, but Nalder proved too much for it, and he soon brought it up over the stern. It died game, by inflicting two or three sharp indentations on Nalder's hand. One of the steerage passengers ascertained the bird's wing length at 5 feet 10 inches. The bird's length was properly measured however, and was found to be upwards of seven feet from tip to tip of its wings.

In the afternoon another albatross was caught, the captor being Hudson, the blacksmith from Pollokshaws. He it was who caught the first dolphin.

In the evening the rain pelted with such a might and the ship was rolling, and driving to and fro everything that got loose.

Latitude 40° 14' S., longitude 76° 41' E.

9 September – A rainy morning, but the ship had been making fair progress during the night, at a speed of about 10½ knots, and the wind, which was on the port, had veered to the starboard quarter.

In the morning I had a discussion with a respected gentleman of the name of Kirkwood, from Maryhill in the north of the city of Glasgow. Kirkwood it was who made a narrow escape from the knife of the Irish cook's mate, for he was the plucky Scot who twice laid low the mad Irishman. He, however, bears along his nose the mark of the knife, and will carry it with him to his grave.

We reminisced of having seen Sir Islay Campbell[15] and his wife Lady Agnes in their carriage as they passed through that village last autumn. She is the daughter of the Marquis of Westminster, and greatly admired by all classes in the neighbourhood.

It was the birthday of our young friend Fred Paul, a nice youth from Bristol, and there was some gaiety on the occasion. But as we were aboard ship and not on *terra firma*, order and discipline must never be forgotten. For instance, if we were on shore we would praise with the chaunt, 'For he's a jolly good fellow', on proposing his health and many happy returns of the day.

That frivolity and hilarity would be rather out of place in the ship's cuddy or chief cabin. In the sanctity attached to the quarter deck of a man-of-war, our Sovereign lady the Queen is assumed to be therever present. A certain degree of respect was also associated with the principal cabin or saloon of a ship of this class. That was respected among the forward passengers and the sailors.

None of the latter ever cross the threshold on any duty, but they instinctively uncovered their heads, just as the captain, officers, and crew would salute on the quarter deck of a Queen's ship. It would, therefore, be unseemly if bursts of boisterous merriment were heard to issue from that sanctuary, which is presumed to afford an example of decorum to the rest of the ship.

It was twilight when two officers emerged, as a torrent of rain was buffeting us, and the second officer told me that he expected squally weather. Looking to the signs to the westward, a seaman like him had his reasons for such thoughts. As someone once remarked, it took a man much of his natural life to understand the weather. Books would not lend the knowledge.

Latitude 40° 38' S., longitude 81° 40' E. We must therefore now be in the southern waters of the Indian Ocean. The wind has got more astern, as we shall soon discover by the rolling.

10 September – A stormy day, and we have had a night of it. Up to half past five o'clock this morning, it blew strongly with occasional showers of hail; but at that hour a fierce squall struck the ship, carried away the mizzen topgallant sail, and split the lower fore studding sail.

Most people were roused from their slumbers, and quite a few left their berths. My boy and I were not disturbed, as was the good fortune too of one or two other ladies and gentlemen in the saloon. All hands were, as a matter of course, called up to shorten sail.

When I awoke about six, I heard the gale roaring amidst the shrouds with a sound louder than any we have yet experienced on our voyage. The motion was not as violent as might have been expected, because the ship was driving at a furious rate through the sea, as if it had no time to veer either to the right or to the left.

I rose and looked out. The sail had been reduced to the foresail reefed, single reefed foretopsail, fullmainsail, and the mizzentopsails close reefed.

Neither the captain nor Mr. Woolley, the first officer, came down to breakfast. They, along with Valentine, were intently occupied on deck. When there was a general call, it was the duty of the third officer to look after the mizzenmast; the second officer took charge of the main, and the boatswain of the foremast.

As I was looking up to the forerigging with a book in my hand, and off my guard, my feet went from me, and, as an Aberdonian lady of old said, I fell 'bra and saft'. I was in no hurry to rise until I had disposed of my book about my person. Who should come to my aid, thinking me disabled, but the Irish cook's mate whom I have already mentioned more than once.

Poor fellow, I could not help feeling sorry for him. He was now doing his duty steadily as a seaman, and took his turn at the wheel with the others.

The Aberdonian lady to whom I have referred above, was walking home from a tea party with a near relative of my own one evening, some seventy years ago, when it was not quite respectable to use the finely expressive Scottish dialect. They had mistaken their way, the night being dark, and both suddenly tripped over a low wall. The lady said to my friend, 'I dinna ken fou you are aff, lassie, but as for me, I've fa'en bra and saft in Nelly Tamson's midden.'[16]

This was not exactly my fate when I came down, but I rubbed shoulders with the cook's slush tub.

Later, there was not a sail set on the mizzen, and very little elsewhere, as it blew so hard. We had two men at the wheel, and the prospect of another squally, rolling night.

We are in latitude 41° 7' S., longitude 86° 3' E.

11 September – I guessed, as those Yankees would say, when I awoke today, that we were lurching 'tarnation hard'. Showers of hail had prevailed throughout the night, with squalls, but our good captain's countenance was serene when he joined us at breakfast, which satisfied me that the night had been satisfactory in a seaman's eyes; or, in other words, that we were going tidily on our course with the wind on our starboard beam, and making from 10 to 10½ knots.

The sea was worth looking at today, it rolled so majestically. Still one had to watch out when moving about, for in one lurch I found myself holding onto the doctor, who, in his turn, held on to Mr. Woolley, with whom steady is ever the word. It was very cold, for we were far south, and we kept both the cuddy doors shut.

The meridian is a mystic hour. It is the hour when, according to the approved tables, the sun must be sighted to calculate the longitude, and, according to the time-honoured rites of Neptune, it is also the eight bells, or close of the forenoon watch, which means with most, a glass of beer.

In such latter duty were some most legitimately engaged at the lower end of the saloon, when suddenly booms forth the cry, 'Three men to the wheel', two having been already stationed there.

A man with a child in his arms had stupidly set forth on the main deck, without someone else beside him. He was thrown against the spare spars, and the poor child's head struck against the rail. I am happy to say there was no serious injury to the little innocent, as the fall of the man had been broken before the child's collision.

Latitude 40° 32' S., longitude 91° 36' E. We had made a run of about 253 miles.

12 September – The night had been quiet, and the rate about 9½ knots which drew to 10½ by the forenoon. It was fortunate for the invalids, of whom we had several below, that the weather has moderated.

One young man from Scotland was in rather a precarious way, for he was suffering from consumption; but we hoped that he may yet be destined to revive. When the ship rolled heavily those who were delicate or indisposed could scarcely be expected to make any headway, as they could find no rest for the body. To others who were well, the motion was rather pleasant; it was as if they had once more returned to their cradles.

The following is a:

Summary List Of Passengers Per *Ganges*

Chief Cabin	19
Second Cabin	48
Enclosed Steerage	61
Open Steerage (married)	33
Single Women	13
Single Men	54
Total	**228**

These 228 have been thrown together from various parts of England, Ireland, and Scotland, with two from Jersey, and one from the Isle of Man. Many of the English counties were represented amongst us. I know of Middlesex (of course), Kent, Essex, Lincolnshire, Devon, Wiltshire, Lancashire, Yorkshire, Warwickshire, Gloucester, Somerset, Shropshire, Herefordshire, and Wales.

I think our Irish were principally from Ulster, though we have a few from Dublin. And turning to Scotland, the great majority hailed from Lanarkshire and Renfrewshire, but Dumbarton, Ayrshire, Argyll, Edinburgh, Perth, Aberdeen, Stirling, Forfar, and Kincardine counties, with the Island of Coll, were also represented.

Among our crew we have denizens of Guernsey, Germany, Denmark, Canada, United States, Sweden, and Holland; but fully two-thirds are British.

The Guernsey men served aboard H.M.S. *Hero*, 90 guns, which has been in the Clyde, and, conveyed the Prince of Wales to and from America in 1860, though if his Royal Highness could have dispensed with his rank, he would have been more comfortable in the *Persia* steamship, as he had a very tedious return voyage in the *Hero*, which was accompanied by the *Ariadne* screw frigate.

On that occasion Commodore Maury,[17] of U.S. Navy, but now with his gallant compatriots the Confederates, and distinguished for his nautical and meteorological science, was consulted on the part of Her Majesty. He gave what proved to be the correct causes for the detention of His Royal Highness on the deep.

Another of our sailors, long old Jacob, a Dane, served on board the *Royal Albert*, 121 guns, in the Black Sea during the Crimean War. I recollected having viewed that vessel on the stocks at Woolwich, in 1849, when it was considered the largest ship in the world; but its dimensions had since been eclipsed, by the *Great Eastern*.[18] The *Royal Albert* had the reputation of being laboursome in a lively sea.

The wind strengthened during the course of the day, and the ship ran beautifully along under most of her square sails, including fore and main royals, with studding-sails, cross-jack, and trysail. After dinner, a sea struck us on the starboard or weather beam, and sent such a cloud of foam along her quarter; but we shipped nothing but spray, as we were light and high out of the water. The order was immediately given to take in the royals and trim the after-yards. The wind continued to rise, and additional sail had to be taken in. The chain of the main topgallant sail snapped during the evening, but the sheet was soon set again.

At night it became more quiet, and, at half past eight, we were seated most comfortably in the saloon, Tom Sutton sat among the ladies, with my little Sally, who was an especial favourite with him, at his side, and peals of laughter echoed around the table as he amused his audience.

Latitude 40° 26' S., longitude 96° 32' E. We have run no less than 1,627 miles during the last week.

13 September, Sunday – Last night, as a party of our young men were engaged at a game of playing cards, a heavy lurch came and swept the cards from the table, along with the stakes, the biscuit tray, and everything that was upon it. Such mishaps were of too frequent occurrence to excite much attention, far less any sympathy.

The night had been dry and quiet, and, what was better, the wind favourable, which carried us onward about 11 knots, a speed that was kept up during the day.

In the afternoon I saw an elderly female make a rather narrow escape. She had incautiously seated herself on the spare spars at the lee side, and immediately below the halyards of the maintop staysail. A lurch had taken the wind out of the sheet when the halyards slackened, and the block twice swept within an ace of her head. A near miss is as good as a mile.

In the evening the captain – of whom we had seen comparatively little for the last day or two, he having been so busy on deck – gave us an account of a voyage he made from Calcutta to Demerara with 600 coolies.[19]

They were horribly filthy, rendering the decks even worse than a pig-sty, until they were brought into some state of discipline by means none of the gentlest, but the most efficient under the circumstances. At best, however, the squalor and effluvia were most repulsive.

In the course of the voyage, with that secrecy characteristic of their race, they had hatched a conspiracy to murder the officers and crew, and take possession of the ship. They chose the most opportune period, when one portion of the crew were aft preparing to swab the decks, and the remainder forward, with the darkies[20] thus placed between them, and cutting off the communication. They broke into the fire-wood store, each arming himself with a stave about three feet long. Thus equipped, they made a rush aft.

The captain was coming out of his cabin smoking a cigar, when he met the purser, who told him that the coolies had risen, and which was soon too evident. The rebels, instead of rushing in at once, as a wise wicked woman of their number had advised them to do, commenced to parley.

The captain and our captain, who was the first officer, managed to get their revolvers; the crew became alive to the crisis, and pointed the muzzles of two of the ship's guns forward, although there was no time to load. That division of the crew who were forward contrived to join their comrades aft by getting along the channels.

The game was then up with the coolies, for they were endeavouring to make terms for larger rations of rice, although they were much better supplied than they had been in their own land.

Nothing but unconditional submission was accepted, and which they saw cause to grant, as the crew was quite ready for a tussle with them, and weapons had since been brought into requisition. Our captain then went forward, accompanied by the second officer, the latter with pistol in hand, and several sailors bearing the manacles.

He seized one of the ringleaders and made him stand and quietly get on his bracelets, the second officer holding a pistol to his head during the operation. They were all fairly cowed.

Poor wretched creatures, their filthy habits sometime subsequently produced malignant fever among them, and there were no more thoughts of mutiny. Many of them died; indeed when one was seen to stretch himself on deck he seldom arose again, unless when taken up to be thrown overboard.

We have gained latitude 40° 32' S., longitude 102° 36' E., and made an excellent run of 276 miles.

14 September – Another quiet night, but the wind fell off towards morning, and we were only making 6 knots. At the same time the ship rolled more than if we were going at 12 knots. It was such a perpetual motion that I really know do not how we shall feel when we once more find ourselves on land.

I suspect it will be a strange and not over pleasant feeling at first, especially during the night when lying on a camp bed, and wanting the rock and lullaby of the world of waters around us.

Man truly was a creature of habit, but, unlike when we were ashore, we were destined to be constantly looking after our legs. Many a day I have had to wash and dress with my lower limbs jammed up as best I could, which, of course, is the ordinary lot of the thousands who annually traversed a great portion of the world's oceans.

In the forenoon my genial friend Thomas Sutton, Esquire – who has passed thousands sterling through his hands annually, is by way of occupation engaged in checking some of the accounts of his brother, Spencer Sutton, our purser.

He was amidst the items which were comprised under the heading of medical comforts to the more delicate or indisposed of the forward passengers. He made a running commentary as he went along. At one point he exclaimed – 'Mutton broth for one lady passenger on Monday, Tuesday, Wednesday, and three succeeding days – why, I wonder she has not grown ashamed to look a sheep in the face.'

Tom was getting better in his health, for latterly he fell a victim to the incessant toil in the chief supervision of extensive works, quarries included. In early youth he had to step into the shoes of his deceased father – whose remains hundreds accompanied to the grave – and be a prop to his family; his widowed mother, and brothers and sisters alike.

The wind freshened in the course of the afternoon, and we came up to 7 or 8 knots, which we reckoned slow work for the ship, after her gallant performances under the rousing gales which carried us around the Cape, and finally into the Southern Ocean.

There is little probability that we will come upon any vessel in these latitudes; indeed, I suspected that our first communication with the world will be when we near Auckland, and were spotted by the pilot.

The order would then be to man the foreyards, so as to back the sails and allow the pilot to come aboard. Very likely, after a shake of his fist, the first question will be – 'Has the *Ida Zeigler* arrived?' That was considered a crack ship. She got out of the Thames the day before the *Ganges*, and must have attained some headway of us, for we did not sight her in the English Channel.

If the *Ida* had taken a more southerly course than our captain had chosen, we may beat her, as she would have encountered strong winds, which would not admit of carrying much canvas.

Latitude 41° 7' S., longitude 107° 40' E., and a run of 233 miles. Temperature, about 58F.

15 September – A bra' morning, with the atmosphere milder than we have experienced for some time; however, we had no wind, and our good ship rolled lustily and lazily.

I had a talk today with Mr. Kemp, to whom I have previously referred as having been in the Crimea, and one of the Railway Brigade. I was mistaken, for I later found out that he was one of the gallant Scots Fusiliers.

He, with his wife and family, were in the second cabin, and I have no doubt would do well in the colony, for he was a very steady, intelligent, respectable man, who had reaped the full advantage of his military training; moreover, he had a powerful athletic frame.

And speaking of military training, I know no better school than the army or navy for a man who is well disposed to his fellow men and resolved to do his duty. I remember Sir James Duke,[21] who, like Joseph Hume,[22] came from my own native town, and who said on one public occasion, when he was Lord Mayor of London, that he traced his success in life to the habits of punctuality he had acquired when acting in a civil capacity on board a man of war. Truly, salt water teaches a man manners.

Out here on the southern ocean we stood no nonsense – no logomachies about liberalism, equality, and the rights of man. The captain is our chief, and his orders must not be questioned. From the first officer downwards the ready response to every order was 'Ay, ay, sir.'

Even in the stewards bar that principle of salutary subordination prevailed. The chief steward, Mr. Neale, and highly he was respected by us all, was sirred by the second steward Bill, an obliging man; and Bill in his turn was sirred by Tom, the third steward. Out of that discipline and respect to lawful authority was generated method, order, and comfort.

The evening was quiet, and therefore our progress rather slow.

Latitude 41° 24' S., longitude 110° 16' E.

16 September – Smooth water, and a lovely day – it could have passed for a September day in Scotland, and for a winter day in Malta, as Mr. Stopford told us, and he knew that island well, for his father had held a high command there

When I rose I almost forgot I was at sea, and might have fancied that I was in snug quarters in Glasgow's Albion hotel, and about to look forth on the busy Trongate.

There was a gentle but steady breeze, out of which we were drawing about 8½ knots; but be our speed what it may, this was an enjoyable day to all, save Captain Funnell, Mr. Woolley, and Mr. Valentine, who would have a strong wind, and the ship to go like 'blazes' before it.

It was pleasant to see some of the ladies below, who were invisible for a few days, now coming on deck, having recovered from their indisposition. Generally, there were more passengers walking the deck today than I had seen for some considerable time.

There is one poor lad, to whom I have already alluded, and who lay in the steerage cabin in a consumptive state. I fear, much fear there would be no disembarkation for him. His name is Kirkwood, and he comes from Kirkintilloch, attended by his father, a quiet, respectable old man.

Last Sunday afternoon I descended into the steerage and had a talk with the father, as he stood by the berth of the son. The former told me that he did not expect that his son would ever recover, but that he would be thankful if he had him ashore, where, he may have quiet consummation.

I saw one of the dogs of Mr. Willan, the Yorkshire farmer, running about the main deck, and muzzled, according to an order which applies to all curs, however quiet and harmless. She was a nice looking animal; but though our English fellow subjects aboard considered her a pure collie, I rather thought that she was a cross, with a dash of the setter in her blood, and for which she may be none the worse.

Talking of muzzling dogs, I may say it would be fine if some passengers would muzzle that unruly member of the human body, the tongue. If not for their own sakes, at least for that of the children running among their feet. It was only the other day, when some one asked my little Yorkshire friend, Jonas Willan, where his father was; to which query Jonas, only three, or, at most, four years of age, laconically answered, 'Dom'd if I know.' A ship on a long voyage is not the best place for a school of industrial language.

At two o'clock in the afternoon, the log indicated 9½ knots, on a smooth sea. Latitude 41° 43' S., longitude 116° 7' E.

17 September – At midnight, I slipped up to the quarter deck to see Mr. Woolley, who was on the watch. The wind was dead aft, the mainsail and cross-jack hauled up, and the ship running at 8 knots, with clear weather. Early in the morning the speed had increased to 10 knots, at which we were smoothly running this afternoon.

Today I made an inspection of the boats of the *Ganges*, and found them in fine trim. Being for this voyage a passenger ship, and hence coming under the relative acts and statutory regulations, we have on board an adequate complement of boats.

There is the longboat, which lies firmly braced on the top of the round house, or forward enclosed second cabin, in which the cook's galley and bakery are also situated. Then comes the jollyboat, the two pinnaces, and the two lifeboats, the two latter being respectively suspended from the davits on the port and starboard quarters, fully equipped, and all ready for lowering.

As the *Ganges* will proceed to Calcutta for a cargo of cotton and other produce after departing Auckland, and cannot expect to have many, if any, passengers, there will be no occasion for more than the long and two other boats. The remaining three will be sold wherever a good market offers.

Inspecting the boats brought to mind my boyhood, when, at 11 years of age I learned to scull upon a crazy dinghy rejoicing in the illustrious title of the *Bellerophon*,[23] which hailed from the romantic little port of Aberdour, on the Fife shore. It had been named after the old 74 gun vessel which received Napoleon.

One day, while sojourning at that favourite watering-place, five of us planned an expedition to the island of Inchcolm,[24] about a mile and a half to the westward of the harbour. We had the precaution not to take the 'bellie', as she was familiarly termed, but a larger boat called the *Dunearn*, in compliment to James Stuart,[25] then of that place, who shot the son of Johnson's 'Bozzy' in an unhappy duel.

The professed object of our adventure was commerce, one of our party wishing to purchase a rabbit from the stock of Sergeant Howie, who with his family were the sole inhabitants of the island. Our outward voyage was easy – we beached our boat, and proceeded to the old Abbey.

A rabbit was produced by one of the Sergeant's daughters, and 9d agreed upon as the price, when the owner rued, and, stroking its ears, said, 'I canna pairt wi't.'

But the intended purchaser was not to be baulked, and resolved that if he could not achieve his end by fair means he would have recourse to foul means.

What could the rest of us do but second his resolve? Accordingly, when the coast was clear, we waited until the rabbits came out of their retreat, which was a hole in an apartment of the venerable and ruinous structure.

Our four-footed foes were, however, too many for us, as we no sooner entered the place on our foray than they rushed to their keep. I saw that this system of tactics would never do, and I therefore advised my comrades not to look to the rabbits, but to make a dash for the hole, and thus cut off their retreat.

A rabbit was soon thus caught, and thrust into the pocket of one of our companions. It was now our turn to beat a retreat and regain our boat, which had now reached the dignity of a piratical cruiser. Lo and behold, the tide had ebbed, and our craft was high and dry! To aggravate our anxieties, the wind had risen, and with it the sea.

Where there is a will there is a way, and in our felonious circumstances we might truly say that we were between the Devil and the deep blue sea. By our united efforts we at length got the *Dunearn* afloat. Fortunately it was a good boat, and two went to each oar, while I, as being the youngest and smallest of the party, was placed at the tiller.

We had a tussle before we regained Aberdour harbour, for the wind was nearly ahead, and more than once did one fine fellow they called Rob Baxter shout to me the order, 'Keep her head well up to the sea,' – an order the importance of which I soon understood.

I recollected, long afterwards, having a somewhat analogous adventure on land. One day, when walking across Corstorphine Hill, near Edinburgh, I saw a sailor running after some white object which was bobbing before him.

He managed to get near to it, and clapped his hat upon it. It proved to be a ferret; and when I reached the spot poor Jack was in a quandary about how to secure his prize, for if he lifted the hat he might either let the animal escape or get his hand bitten in attempting to retain it. I considered the state of matters, and then ordered the sailor to produce his handkerchief, and spread it on the ground close to his hat, which was then cautiously drawn upon the sheet, and the four corners braced over the crown of the hat. The sailor, after warmly thanking me for my counsel, departed exulting in his capture.

At six o'clock in the evening it was beginning to blow, and we rolled most jollily. As the wind was dead astern, there was no use in carrying much square sail, as one sail would shake the wind out of another. On the mizzen mast we had only the lower topsail; on the mainmast there were the two tops, the topgallant, and royals; and on the foremast the foresail and two tops. In that trim we scudded along at 11 knots. In one wild lurch down came the carcass of a sheep from the skids.

That caused great merriment among the forward passengers, who set to bleating and making such a din until the loud tones of Woolley were heard, ordering quiet. We were yesterday in the same longitude as Cape Leuwin, which is about the westernmost point of Australia. Today we were about 420 miles off the Australian coast, so that we considered ourselves as again nearing the land.

It was the first anniversary of the battle of Antietam,[26] in Maryland, where McClellan, on the Federal side, gained some credit, and General Lee, in command of the Confederates, lost none – for he chose his own ground.

We sometimes wonder how that lamentable struggle is now progressing, as the course of events for the last three months is as yet a sealed book to us. We sat here doing our best to read, write, and amuse ourselves by the cabin lamps, which swung to and fro in great style – at one moment shedding the light on our page, the next leaving us in the shade.

Latitude 42° 34' S., longitude 117° 51' E. – which gave a satisfactory run.

18 September – We had a nice breeze in the morning on the starboard quarter, and we had been going from 10 to 10½ knots during the night. We ran 251 miles yesterday, and, as Mr. Woolley told me a little ago, our work today had been 242 miles.

At that rate we cannot be very long of once more seeing land, and finally reaching our destination. The last land that was visible to us was the coast of Devonshire, when we left Old England on the lee; and Melbourne will be about 800 miles distant from where we are now.

Not knowing what is going on in the world at present, we were given to note the events of the past. This was the anniversary of the birth of that old Trojan, Samuel Johnson – a man during whose time it was worth knowing. No wonder that he was the god of Boswell's[27] idolatry.

He scarcely found the same favour in the eyes of his old fashioned father, Lord Auchinleck,[28] who somewhere says – 'What think ye o' our Jamie? He was first ta'en up with a land-louping scoundrel named Paoli,[29] and noo he's in tow wi' an auld dominie, Doctor Johnson, that keepit a skule, and ca'd it an academie.'[30]

Something very neat was also said on the same theme by an accomplished friend of my own, whose picture I have on board, as it appeared in the *Illustrated London News*, on the occasion of a splendid tribute rendered to his integrity, talent, and public services. He said that he liked when Johnson sat down to his copious libations of tea, 'because they made Johnson talk, and kept his reporter, Boswell, sober'.

Little did I once think that I would be jotting down this reminiscence, among many of my excellent friends, when tossing about far off in the great Southern Ocean! The *Ganges* rolled this night; but what matters? – the wind is fair, and she goes rejoicing on her course.

Latitude 43° 32' S., longitude 123° 12' E.

19 September – A fine, rousing wind this morning, directly onto the port quarter, and she travelled at fully 13 knots. Faster than the fastest of the stage coaches in England in the good olden times, before the iron horse came to puff, snort, bestride, and veil merry England, and old Scotland into the bargain, as if the soil was all its own.

I entertained a certain sort of respect for a certain staunch Conservative, one by the name of Colonel Sibthorpe, who to the last travelled from London to his country seat in his carriage-and-four, having vowed never to embark upon a railway. Just as countrymen of my own have preferred to avoid the seven-mile sail from Leith to Kinghorn, having vowed never to go home over the waters of the Forth again as long as the bridge at Stirling remained intact.

At 12 o'clock, noon they again commenced the rehearsal of the music for the Sunday service, and as like the preceding week, the scene was rather strange. The fine, manly frame of Mr. Green stood down at the foot of the table, pouring out a glass of beer; Mr. Stopford was perusing Massinger's play, *A New Way to Pay Old Debts*;[31] and the Captain and the Doctor grinned at me, who, in my turn, grinned back at them. Tom Sutton sat at the other extremity, and threw his rich voice into the song.

The day was dull – one of dead reckoning; but the wind whistled merrily through the rigging. What more could we wish? It was true the music halts a little as the vessel lurches, but we cannot expect to have an accomplished musician out here with Glasgow's City Hall organ.

I have heard that excellent instrument several times, but not on the night when Tommy Sayers[32] gave an exhibition there, along with his colossal foe, Jack Heenan[33] – whom I really believe he would have quilted [knocked out] on that memorable morning at Farnborough (17th April, 1860), had the fight been allowed to proceed.

While at dinner, the wind suddenly veered from the port to the starboard quarter, and blew strongly, carrying the ship beautifully along at 13 knots. She did give some sweeping lurches, and I saw the carcass of a sheep which was swinging wildly about give a poor fellow who came in its way a good thump on the shoulder.

We were carrying royals and stunsails, and, as the boatswain Mister Lee said, the *Ganges* was never put through her mettle as she had been during her present voyage.

Latitude 44° 45' S., longitude 128° 46' E., having been an uncommonly good run since yesterday.

20 September, Sunday – During the night the wind had been blowing steadily on the starboard beam, and the rate has been from 9 to 10 knots. We were far south now, and the weather was cold, the thermometer below 50F.

During the morning the snow came down, as a Scotchman said, as thick as buttermilk. It then turned to rain, and the weather was rather inclement. Still the wind was fair, and strengthening, and that was the main consideration. We were able to carry ample sail, and sped along at from 12 to 13 knots.

Heavy showers of hail came down, but the sun broke forth at intervals. One pelt covered the decks, when all, including some of the sailors who were off duty, had a regular snow-ball skirmish. As the wind was only slightly abaft the beam, our outer and inner jib filled well.

In the journal of his voyage to Auckland, Buchanan reminisced of his boyhood summer days, when with friends he often roamed around Leith Harbour admiring the many sea-going vessels of the merchant and Royal Navy fleets that visited the port. This sketch shows the harbour as it would have been in the early years of the 19th century, and how it would have looked around the time of Buchanan's youth. Reproduced with acknowledgment to Peter Stubbs www.edinphoto.org.uk

Yesterday, when the wind was on the quarter, they kept flapping about; still I should not have liked to have seen them down, as they serve as a safeguard to prevent the ship from beaching to, or coming too close to the wind, as it did one night, when we lost some of our sails, and the man was dashed from the wheel.

We were about 600 miles from Melbourne, and should be as far east as that town tomorrow. At the rate we were going, ten days would take us to Auckland, or within the 100 days from England. We have yet to run four or five degrees south, and we may expect that it will be precious cold in that latitude.

At six o'clock in the evening Mr. Valentine, the officer on watch, entered the cabin to announce to the captain that poor young Kirkwood was delivered from all his earthly troubles, having expired within the preceding two minutes.

He was sensible to the last – indeed, was rather lively today, having fancied that he was better, but the symptoms were most deceptive, as Mr. Welby, the surgeon, informed his father in the course of the forenoon.

He was to be consigned to the deep tomorrow. His relatives, naturally for them, desired that a chest should be made in the usual manner for the body. The captain offered them the materials, but, for reasons that I need not specify, strongly advised them to abide by the ordinary usage at sea, which they did.

At night the moon and stars shone out, and the ship was going at 12 knots.

Latitude 45° 40' S., longitude 134° 50' E.

21 September – Today was the 118th anniversary of the Battle of Prestonpans,[34] when our gallant Highlanders fought with Sir John Cope's English Dragoons, now the 14th (the King's) Hussars – a piece of information that I have been good humouredly giving to some of our English friends out here for their edification.

When the day dawned I felt by the heavy rolling of the ship that the wind had fallen off, and left us heaving on the swell. It had gone on the stern; however we made 10 knots during the greater part of the night, and were at 10 a.m. going at 8, with clear weather, but cold, the temperature reading 52F in the captain's cabin.

Yesterday the ship gave one specially violent lurch, when I saw a lady fly past the poop binnacle and go down. Fortunately she was not hurt. I was standing at the time at the lee side poop rail, so that it did not trouble me. I believe that it would have upset anyone who had been caught unprepared.

At 11 o'clock in the morning, all who were able assembled in the waist of the ship, that being the appointed hour for the burial of young Kirkwood, aged 19. The British ensign was hoisted at the peak, and the boatswain, sailmaker, and two seamen stationed at the lee gangway, over which the body was to be lowered into the sea.

There was, as a matter of course, an eager crowd clustered around, the women not being among the most backward. The Rev. Mr. Smith, the clergyman of the deceased and his father, attended, as also Mr. Anderson, who was to officiate, Mr. Smith having not been strong enough yet for that duty.

The first officer gave the order to clear the gangway, when the body was brought aft from the fore hatchway on a shutter, carried on the shoulders of four men, and wrapped around with the Union Jack. It was then, on the pall being removed, lowered over the side, when a few verses of the 90th Psalm (the *Domine Refugium* of the Church of England burial service) were given out and sung. A short prayer was then offered up, the order was given to let go, and the body vanished into the waters of the great deep.

The father and relatives stood by, the tears trickling down the honest manly countenance of the old man. In this way ended the ceremony – the decks were soon cleared, and matters resumed their natural way.

We have had two deaths and two births on board, for I was not aware until the other day that a child was born in the steerage before the ship cleared out of the London docks. The parents were a respectable couple from the West of Scotland, and have already been in Australia. The girl was named Ganges, after the ship, and as yet has never known any other home, or ever been on dry land.

At two o'clock in the afternoon the wind had sprung seaward, and we went along at 12 knots, with a heavy rain subsequently having drenched the decks. At night the wind was still astern, with the speed from 9 to 10 knots.

Latitude 45° 53' S., longitude 140° 40' E.

22 September – The night has been quiet, with a nice little breeze; but today the weather was rather cloudy, with occasional showers and little wind.

There were signs of coming events among us; a pig was killed last night, of which it was hoped the ship's agents will be able to share, when they come on board at Auckland, for meat will keep well in these latitudes.

Several were now seated around me busy writing letters to go home to their far distant friends. Tom Sutton was at the top of the table, in the captain's chair, and engaged in checking accounts; but that occupation was not so arduous as to prevent him from now and then pitching into the cabin parson, who sat beside me with his dictionary, poring over words for his verses. The day had continued quiet, with the speed varying from 8 to 9 knots.

At eight o'clock at night, we were making 11 knots, with the wind astern. The captain and I rather surprised a lady today, by telling her that every incident on the voyage must be chronicled in the ship's log, under a penalty, which journal is submitted to the Customs authorities at Auckland, and that, among other items of information, was the fact that she had come to a black eye. Of course she soon saw the joke.

I had a talk with Mr. Kirkwood, who lost his son on Sunday. The poor lad died almost imperceptibly – no active pain – as if the span of life had been attenuated to a thread. He possessed a certificate for a land grant of 40 acres.

On the general principle, and according to the law of England, which now controls us, every right vested in the son would accrue to the father, unless that, in carrying out the colonial policy, there may be a local law which would render the privilege of the deceased void.

However, it was probably of little concern, for these free grants were not held in any high estimation with us. I have a right to an allotment of 160 acres, on behalf of self and family. I only wish they were in Clydesdale instead of the wilds of New Zealand, and I would not be out here. But it was as well to possess the right, for which only 10s.[35] per 40 acres is paid down; and who can tell what may turn up?

Latitude 47° 2' S., longitude 144° 30' E. Temperature, 57F in the forenoon.

23 September – Today was splendid – we just could not have desired one better. There was a strong favouring wind blowing on the starboard beam – quite a rattling breeze. We ran at 13 knots, and the sun shone brightly.

As I looked over the lee bulwarks, the sight was very fine; around us was the lovely blue of the ocean, intermingled at intervals with the white that came running down from the crests of the billows. Along the port bows there was a sheet of foam that would have more than spanned Glasgow's spacious Buchanan Street. No artist could have fully portrayed the grandeur of the scene.

The *Ganges* dashed through the waters too rapidly to allow her time for her rolls and capers; but a sea will occasionally strike her on the weather scudder, which she saucily turned aside like a rejected suitor, when he, the slighted, takes his revenge by throwing a deluge across her waist.

A few minutes since, espying the hem of the garment of our black-eyed matron, *vide* my log of yesterday, at the saloon entrance, I went to greet her with the compliments of the morn, and inquire for her worthy husband, who had been complaining.

She was decked out in a silk gown, which, in the state of the weather, I did not consider over-prudent. Little time elapsed before a sea came which flew over the main deck. I saw the windy thick spray. I rushed to the cuddy door and pulled the lady within, all dripping with the brine, like Neptune, with his trident, on emerging out of his submarine villa.

I saw it was no case of combing down, and accordingly the lady had to go to her cabin for a thorough overhaul and refit. Two young fellows were reclining intent on their cards, when the sea came and fairly won the trick, for the cards were saturated and dispersed.

Mr. Woolley, as on a previous occasion, this morning also met his share of the sea, and had to rigout anew from top to bottom. Little did Woolley, that fine tough little man, care for such mishaps.

As the day advanced the wind rose, and at half past 7 in the evening it blew with a will. Earlier, I was standing on the main deck, at a little after four o'clock in the afternoon, when a fierce squall struck the ship. In a twinkling the forecastle was almost hidden from my view by the clouds of spray that were flying over it.

Instantly all was cries and bustle on deck, in the hurry to take in sail. One seaman had not distinctly heard, or misapprehended the order to let go the main topgallant halyards, when a voice thundered forth from the poop – 'Damn my eyes, look alive, am I to sing out half a dozen times?' It was no time to be over-particular on the choice of language.

All of us, men and boys, who happened to be on deck, instinctively lent a hand in helping to pull the rope. Capt. Marshall and I were tugging at the same line, and cheered on the young fellows. How the ship did begin to roll! One lurch to leeward brought the lee scuppers on a level with the sea which came over the bulwarks, and she seemed to dance like a fishing yawl out at sea. Twice or thrice a sea struck us on the starboard quarter, when I distinctly felt her frame quiver with the shock.

I was told by one of the officers that we were to have a stormy night. In the meantime matters went on with us as usual, only that I had to lash the cabin lamp at my end of the table. The captain had then entered, and made my Sally feel the cold of his hands. He had no sooner gone out by the opposite door than a sea struck us with a loud rebound, sweeping over the deck; and it staggered us all, but only for a moment. I suspected, however, as by the look of the weather, it was the forerunner of others.

How the wind did howl. Still, our tars, when working the pump about an hour since, had their chaunt. This evening it ran, 'Row, boys, row for California. For I've been told there's plenty of gold, in the banks of Sacramento.' It was by no means unmusical as heard amidst the roar of the elements.

I had only written the above few lines when bang went another sea on our starboard quarter, and the ship's after bell tolled when it had no business to toll. It swept over the quarter deck, and I heard it on the skylight above my head, which, however, did not go (I mean the skylight, not my head); but it was indeed intended not to subject it to another such trial, for immediately afterwards I heard the carpenter hammering down the canvas that had been placed around it.

At half past 11 o'clock at night, I remembered what the captain had told me an hour earlier that we had suffered the roughest night we had experienced since we left England. I scarcely required the information. Half an hour previous about the heaviest sea we have had struck the ship and came over the weather bow. It would have astonished those in the fore steerage as they heard it roll over their hatches, which were, of course, battened down. One consolation was that the night was clear, the moon and stars having shone out, and we had only three tops and foresail set.

Latitude 48° 18' S., longitude 148° 52' E.

24 September – A little before midnight last night I became aware that the gale was moderating, and I was soon confirmed in my surmise by seeing Capt. Funnell come down in his storm gearing, and seat himself beside me for a few minutes rest. He said that the worst had passed. I hoped we would not get worse than that worst.

This roving over ocean only requires a beginning. I will settle down as quietly as I can ashore, and be an industrious and frugal person, as I have always been compelled. Still, if Providence spares me, I have felt that the North Isle of New Zealand would not be my endmost sail, although it may be my present journey's end.

I should like to have a run across from New Zealand and its Maoris to Australia. The distance is some 1,200 miles, but it would now cost me no more thought than embarking at the Broomielaw, on board the *Express* for Kilmun,[36] with the company of some good friends.

Today was fine, and all that was bequeathed to us by its rather turbulent predecessor was a bit of a swell. That apt expression, I heard drop from the lips of a skilful seaman, and, what is more, a sincere pious little man, Captain Wilson, of the General Steam Navigation Company's ship, *Trident*.

I sailed with him from London to Granton of Edinburgh in the beginning of last April, and made a beautiful run of 17 hours. On the Sunday evening he had held Sunday worship in the spacious saloon of the *Trident*, he himself officiating as reverend. He devoutly went through the task, reading the Church of England service, and also a portion of the Scripture.

The honest, little, burly seaman also had the Psalmody, and, apologised for the absence of accompanying instruments, owing to the swell (for we were in the Wash at the time). He led off the singing himself, and I cannot say that Captain Wilson exactly came forth as the sweetest of singers; still, I will say that the melody came from the heart.

We shipped more than one sea during the night, but not to any great extent. Most of us knew nothing about it until morning. Today the wind had got astern, and we had ample sail set, but we were making little more than 9 knots.

Earlier in the day, in the forenoon, Mr. Nalder caught a Cape pigeon and Mr. Fred Paul a large sea bird. When we get near New Zealand we may have the chance of capturing a shark.

Latitude 49° 40' S., longitude 155° 0' E.

25 September – A fine morning, with a brisk wind blowing on the port quarter, and every stitch of canvas which was set drawing to the full advantage, and driving on the ship at 11½ knots.

We cannot be very far off the coast of New Zealand; indeed, an agriculturist from Gloucestershire has taken a bet with me that we shall see land at or before 12 o'clock tomorrow. He will be the loser. I have also gained a bet from the purser, who would insist with me that a great man was born on such a date, when I said nay. I managed to procure evidence to convince him that he was wrong.

I may add that those so-called bets are very harmless, for I have always disliked gambling in all its forms, so much so that I never had any problem in avoiding it.

Last night the little sailor boy Edward Lowe, whom I have previously mentioned, came into the cabin to get the time as I was sitting beneath the clock. He was telling me that he has now been several times aloft on the main royalyards helping to let go the sail.

I told him, as I did formerly, to persevere, and he had every chance, if he continued a good boy, to gain an honourable position in his manly calling.

He had finished *Robinson Crusoe*, and returned it to my boy in the same unsoiled state as he received it. I like those tidy habits, and especially as regards books, have often, while perusing a library volume, reproached those who must scrawl in the margin, any shallow thought that found entrance into their still more shallow craniums.

There existed, however, one illustrious and generous man, Lord Jeffrey,[37] who was as unscrupulous about the treatment of the outside of a book as he was critically scrupulous in regard to its inward matter. On one occasion my own departed and respected father lent to him *Cobbet's Cottage Economy*, a work written in the most excellent English, as he had resolved to review it in the *Edinburgh Review*. That eminence of literature, Archibald Constable,[38] of Edinburgh, did not know where to readily find a copy.

Lord Jeffrey, however, did take good care of that little volume, for unwittingly he retained it, and my father's book shelves knew it no more.

What a production is that *Robinson Crusoe*! I have renewed acquaintance with it on board this ship, having gone through it faithfully from the beginning to the end.

Much has been said in more modern times – in this iron utilitarian age – of the advances which have been made in the instruction of youth – of the improved, and, above all, highly moral tone of juvenile literature. So show me, any work so better calculated to attract, to interest, to inform, and to fascinate the youthful mind as is *Robinson Crusoe*. Even the best – and the stories of Miss Edgeworth[39] are excellent – still pale before the immortal work of Defoe, having been, as it has, and I hope is still destined to be, a landmark in the youthful memories of many successive generations.

But I must see what our ship is doing, as a few minutes since she gave a very considerable lurch, and at 12 o'clock noon the wind became loud and strong, with a rising sea. They are hauling aft and reefing the mainsheet, and I hear our tars singing out, 'Haul away, haul away, Joe!'

A sea has struck us on the weatherport, and drenched the berths of those who had unluckily left their ports open. Fortunately for me, I am on the right or leeside today, and my berth is safe.

Eight o'clock in the evening – The weather became more stormy in the course of the afternoon, with a good deal of rain. The dead-lights were clapped on the cabin sky-lights as soon as the lamps were lighted, and the sail has been reduced to the foresail, reefed mainsail, and close-reefed topsails.

We were thus all taut for a blow; but the night grew clearer, and I rather thought that the wind promised to fall. There is, however, a rough, tumbling sea around us. The sheet-rope of the mainsail, was standing so tight and so inviting within two feet of the main deck, that I could not resist laying hold of one of the posts that support the skids, and proceeding to have a skip or two. A lurch soon came and put paid to my gambols, for I was capsized and rolled away to the lee side, rising not a bit the worse.

By way of covering my inglorious fall, I ascribed the mishap to the want of a balancing pole, and which apology was duly logged among the tales to be told to that fine amphibious race, the marines.

8.30, evening – At the moment the ship staggers under another surly bang, and our young friend, Johnnie Hanson, of Essex County, who chanced to be near the water-can, has got regularly sonsed with its contents.

Latitude 50° 13' S., longitude 161° 33' E. Temperature about 55F.

26 September – The wind had not been so high during the night, but there was still a good sea rolling. I was glad for the sake of poor Jack, to learn that a glass of grog was to be served to those who were to be on the middle watch. They would be all the better for it.

During that watch a sea struck the ship and swept over the poop. It was not spray, but, as the second officer said, a regular unbroken bash of water which enveloped him.

The speed was about 10 knots, but this morning we were going at 11, with a fine stiff breeze right aft. We were carrying little sail – on the mizzen there is nothing but the lower top; on the main two tops and topgallant reefed; and on the fore full topsails, foresail, and foretop staysail.

It was all up with my Gloucestershire friend – he had lost his bet, for there will be no land in sight at twelve tomorrow. It was the Island of Auckland they expected to see. That hour now approaches while I write, when he must come down with his bottle of London stout.

Last night, as I was sitting for a minute or two with the captain, Mr. Woolley entered and announced that a flash of lightning had been seen. The captain and his trusty first lieutenant then got hold of the sextant of the latter, and made the cabin lamp for that moment do duty for the sun in their anxiety to obtain a sight.

12 o'clock, noon. – We have discussed the bet. There is of course great anxiety once more to have a glimpse, however distant, of that dark mass they call land. For my own part, I have no great longing or impatience in the matter.

The truth is, that the sight of land will bring many anxieties in its train as to the future, and to me no very pleasing reminiscences as to the past, seeing as the only comfortable season I have spent, within a considerable period, has been on the wide ocean, whether amidst calm or storm. Why, then, should I be pining after shore, or in any violent haste to leave that kindly element on which I have recovered that health and strength which had eventually deserted me on land?

A year has elapsed, exactly on this day, since I entered my dwelling, feeling woundily bad. I did not recross its threshold for days and weeks. Then it was Dr. Easton, the Professor of Materia Medica in Glasgow University, who attended and advised me. If

I go to either end of the world, I would not find better than him whose science and skill are only equalled by his benevolence.

Tom Sutton was at this moment sitting beside me, engaged in writing to his friends in Kent – giving them a little of his Kentish fire. He sympathised with me, and remarked – 'Why, I am deuced comfortable where I am, and care not how long we are before letting go the anchor.' Still, the land will be grateful to not a few, who do not stand the sea well, and more especially to some who are ailing.

In the early part of this evening the weather was thick and rainy, but it was eight o'clock moonlight, though misty in the distance, and we went merrily on at about 12 knots.

Latitude 50° 16' S., longitude 168° 18' E.

27 September, Sunday – It blew strongly in the morning from the westward, and well on to the port beam. The spray flew over the decks as we went pitching along at 11 knots. Last night at ten o'clock we were dashing onward at 14 knots.

It was what we would call a gusty day in Scotland; but we were sitting here very snugly in the saloon, which Mrs. Walby, the lady of our surgeon, had at present entered and caught the table, just in time to save herself from an overthrow, for the ship did tumble in good style.

If any staid citizen from the land was suddenly thrown among us he would think us rather an eccentric community. It was only the other day that a friend got a fall which speedily revealed itself in the shape of a black eye.

Today, immediately before the cabin service, Mr. Lopdell, our parson, met with a similar fate, and looked as if he had figured in the prize ring. He is a good man, and so correct in his walk and conversation that he refuses everything in the form of wine, spirits, beer, and tobacco, although he is most liberal and indulgent to others who do not come exactly up to the same exemplary standard.

One day, lately, I saw one of our sailors looking very poorly. I spoke to him, when he told me that he had been suffering from ague, but was striving to stand to his guns, or keep his watch. He was a native of some place near Toronto, in Upper Canada, and has a dark foreign complexion. I told him that, with the permission of the purser, I would give him a drop of port wine.

I was walking down the saloon on my way outside to him with the little comfort for his infirmity, when I passed our parson sitting studying, with his back to me and his coat pocket most invitingly open. I quietly slipped the flask into his pocket.

I then announced as quietly to Mr. Stopford that I had played my part in the first act of the vaudeville, and I would leave the remainder to him – that is, to put the ladies up to the little stratagem, and then let us have an effective *dénouement*. The harmless practical jest went off finely, no one joining more heartily in the fun than our virtuous parson himself.

About three o'clock the horizon cleared, a beautiful sunshine came forth, but the serenity brought in its wake an unprofitable decrease in the wind. Our speed went down to eight knots. The order was immediately given to clad on more canvas, and up went spanker, topgallant, and also the royals on the main. The ship then came up to ten knots.

As our tars were pulling at one of the braces, old Jacob, the Dane, took the lead in singing some yarn, which ran thus – 'They brought a Frenchman on board a whaler – he had on his Sunday clothes. He did not know his duty, and so they turned him off.'

Jack was not a rhythmical animal – he was easy to satisfy in that respect; still, it was astonishing how well he could smooth down the properties when he came to the vocalisation; and then how hearty and cheering was the sound when the united voices broke forth in the 'We'll all pull together – away O! – away O!'

In the evening the wind, which was slight, got on our port bows and became foul. Still, it was a lovely moonlight night, and almost reminded me of some of those that we had when passing through the tropics, although, of course, the temperature was very different.

Latitude 47° 31' S., longitude 172° 3' E.

28 September – A beautiful calm morning, but with a north and a foul wind, and the yards sharp braced. It was becoming warmer, as the temperature was 59F.

Groups were congregated along the deck in eager converse about the promised land which they expected to reach in the course of this week. It seemed as easy to walk the deck today as if we were not on the Southern Ocean, but embarked on the queen of lakes, Loch Lomond.

I suspect that, if the tourists who were this day careering along the beautiful waters of Loch Lomond, suddenly encountered the petty heaving which now accompanied us, they would imagine that there was some commotion going on beneath their feet.

The Cape pigeons and other birds hovered so close upon the stern that they seemed to say to the *Ganges* – 'Come woo me!' Mr. Green and Mr. Nalder are not loath to take up the challenge and they are leaning over the taffrail with their long hunting whips, intent to get a cut at one of those birds.

I have seen swallows thus brought down on a loch; that of Canonmills, near Edinburgh, where I once got a regular soaking when the ice gave way under me while skating. I had to hold on as best I could, while hearing the cry of 'Rope! Rope!' from some of the adjoining tanneries. By the help of a plucky comrade, with whom I had fought just a few weeks before, I got out, without any such extraneous aid, and said something to the effect that here is a holiday spoiled, and a domestic squall in the offing into the bargain.

At one o'clock in the afternoon I heard a loud ringing order – 'All hands up; about ship' – and I knew well what that meant. At that moment the captain sung out 'Down with the main-tack.' We are going to try and dodge the wind as best we may. Old Chips was hauling away with the rest, and a sober, industrious man he is; but whether it be from his ignorance of the English language, he, being a Prussian, or his indifference as to its niceties, I know not. Certainly from no wicked disposition, he is apt to indulge in rather uncouth speech. Our Chips was industriously sawing away at one of our spars which had snapped in a gale, and letting go a little of his language at the same time, which unluckily hit the ears of the junior Scotch parson outside.

He warned Chips that he would go to a certain place for using certain and improper expressions. All the change he took out of Chips was 'I will be damned if I do.' I believe that this loose mode of talking was with many more a bad – very bad – habit than any incarnate vice or evil in their nature.

In the days of the press-gang,[40] when gallant naval officers appointed to that department had to hunt down honest seamen like felons, they sometimes brought themselves into unpleasant collision with the civil authorities.

A Captain (afterwards Admiral) Laird was in this predicament, for he was summoned to the bar of the Court of Session for having failed to render obedience to an alleged mandate of that Court. On Sir Islay Campbell, the Lord President, calling out the name of Captain Laird, the latter sung out in a loud voice from the back of the Court, 'Here'. He was requested to come forward to the bar.

Instead of passing round by the regular gangway or passage the gallant captain successively jumped over the intervening benches until he alighted at the bar. The charge against him was read, and he was asked what he had to say to it. He simply answered, ' 'Tis a damned lie.'

He was admonished that this was not language to employ within a court of justice. The captain was silent. The celebrated John Clerk[41] gave the captain a pinch of snuff, to show, I presume, that he was influenced by no personal feeling in the performance of his professional duty.

He then proceeded briefly to state the case against the captain, and at the conclusion the latter indignantly snapped his fingers and thumb, exclaiming – 'That, for ye all!' It, however, eventually came out that the order which the captain was said to have disobeyed had not been regularly served upon him. Accordingly, the charge fell to the ground; but Sir Islay Campbell stated that Captain Laird had still to answer for the disrespect which he had that day shown to the Court.

Lord Hermand,[42] who lived to be an aged Judge – for I can remember him very well – had always indulged in a strong and laudable partiality for the naval service. He at this stage came to the rescue, and suddenly struck in – 'My Laird President, Captain Laird has used the language which is indigenous to British seamen. May they continue to use that language, and may they speak it in the face of thunder itself.' Of course, after this honest explosion on the part of Hermand, nothing more was to be said, and Captain Laird came off scot free.

The wind continued foul, and we were making worse than no progress, with mainsail and topsails reefed, for it threatened to blow. Latitude 47°15' S., longitude 176° 7' E.

29 September – A beautiful morning, which seemed to foreshadow the climate which we now must be approximating to, though very slowly, for we are at present well nigh becalmed. I am sorry for our excellent captain; for if ever a navigator taxed his energies and spared not himself to make a rapid passage, it has been Captain Thomas Funnell.

But as our own Burns,[43] into whom I dipped greedily last night, says, the best laid schemes of mice and men, will sometimes go awry; and the Scriptures tell us, that the race is not always to the swift nor the battle to the strong.

When I went upon deck, rather early – for what was the use of wasting the cheerful morn in one's berth? – I saw flocks of seabirds, albatrosses, Cape pigeons &c., swimming along by the side of the vessel, and scrambling for the refuse thrown overboard.

A cluster of the smaller fry had got hold of something, and were contending for the prize when down came a mollyhawk[44] with a fell swoop and bore off with the booty. Ay, thought I, whether it be on sea or on shore, the strong will despoil the weak, and despots will forget that they are but men.

Yesterday my boy caught one of those mollyhawks, a pretty bird, and measuring about seven feet from tip to tip of the wings. The cook had kindly promised him to extract the bone from one of the wings, so that he may preserve some memento of the sport.

A little ago, Fred Paul entered the cabin bearing a long line of sea-weed which had been hooked up; and yesterday afternoon the captain told me that he had seen a bird from the land – indeed, one passenger said to me that he had seen the land this morning, and that several of the sailors had avouched the fact.

I suspect it was a bank of fog. At all events, I do not wish to believe it, for I have a bet that we do not let go the anchor until 12 o'clock on Saturday next.

There were appearances of a breeze – certain streaks in the sky, and 'mares' tails and mackerel scales make lofty ships take down their sails'. The decks were very lively today, as if the prisoners felt they were to be soon let free. Dr. Johnson gave a jail a preference to a ship – for, to his mind, both were places of confinement – but, as he said, people had the chance of being drowned in a ship, a peril from which they were exempt in a jail.

Dr. Johnson was a wise and a good man, but here I must presume to differ with him, for I would rather continue my abode with Captain Funnell in the *Ganges*, than partake of the hospitalities of that respectable and genial gentleman, Governor John Stirling, who was in charge of Glasgow's city jail.

At eight o'clock in the evening I considered that we had had a lovely day, along with a brilliant sunset; indeed, one might have imagined this forenoon that we were once more approaching the tropics. The decks were filled with the passengers, and little Ganges was up with her mother, both parent and child looking remarkably well.

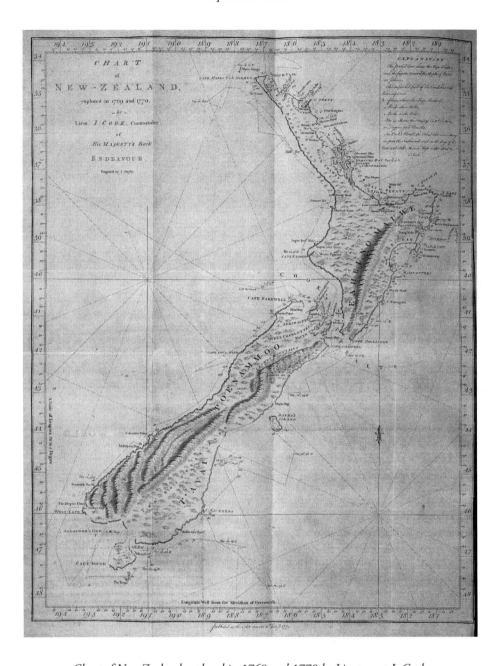

Chart of New Zealand explored in 1769 and 1770 by Lieutenant J. Cook.

When the Ganges *was sailing up the New Zealand coast, David Buchanan paid homage to Captain James Cook, who – while he commanded the barque* Endeavour *– charted the New Zealand coast and claimed the land for the British crown. This chart – dated 1773 – was printed just 90 years before the* Ganges *had literally navigated New Zealand waters in the wake of Cook's historical voyage. From the Rare Voyages Collection, Special printed Collections, courtesy of the Alexander Turnbull Library, Wellington, New Zealand*

I saw the lead ready, but at this rate it would be a while before we took soundings; in fact, we were making no way, or at least very little, for if the ship was answering her helm that was about all.

A sweepstake of 5s. [5 shillings or 25p] each had this day been got up among the cabin passengers, each drawing a particular day, the spoil falling to the one who chanced to hold the day on which the ship may arrive. The land that was thought to be seen would have been the Province of Otago, if anything.

I observed today that there were surviving four fowls, two sheep, and three pigs, the latter in fine condition, for no place is better than a passenger ship for feeding up pigs, as there are so many scraps for their troughs.

Latitude 46° 56' S., longitude 175° 0' E.

30 September – The day was really fine – not too warm; on the contrary, there was a gentle nip along with it. The air was so pure and so fresh.

I took an hour on the main deck before turning in to a jolly good breakfast, both cutlets and mutton chops being served up. We had the wind well forward on the port beam, but were not making above three or four knots, and that not altogether in the right direction.

At one o'clock in the afternoon I heard an order to let go some of the braces, which told me that the wind had shifted for the better, as we had been very close hauled throughout the day; or in other words, jammed too near the eye of the wind.

Little Jonas Willan passed my port at that moment, and a fine boy is he. Poor little fellow, he fell the other day right down the second cabin ladder, and, as the purser said to me, was within an ace of breaking his neck. Jonas was made of good stuff – he got a wild tumble; but, as his father told me this morning, his first reaction when he reached the lower deck, and was gathered up, was 'Where's my caap?' I asked him if he cried, when he got the fall; he turned his little dark eyes down upon me through the port, and indignantly exclaimed, 'Naay.'

These are the boys that I 'loikes', as Jonas would say, and I have left a dear little nephew behind me who comes up to that standard. He may yet follow me with honourable and industrious intent.

Later, at eight o'clock in the evening, the wind had at last come upon our port quarter, and we then moved along at 9½ knots, and expected to be up to 11 by ten o'clock. Yesterday, we only progressed 30 miles, and we have several hundred still to go, although to us that now seems such a short distance.

Latitude 46° 20' S., longitude 174° 40' E.

---

1. A reference to one of the notorious leaders of the Border reivers, who were family clans of warriors and cattle thieves who terrorised the border country of Scotland and England from the late Middle Ages until the early 17th century. The Scottish novelist Sir Walter Scott published a book, *Scottish Border Minstrelsy*, which renewed public interest in the name and deeds of Jock Elliot and other reiver leaders.

2. The Leith smacks, or cutters as they were sometimes named, were vessels of about 200 tons which carried cargo or passengers or sometimes both, and operated around the British east coast and the nearer European ports.

3. Due to the 1914–18 war with Germany, the British altered the British name from the German Ocean to the North Sea.

4. Oliver Goldsmith, 1730–74, Irish playwright, novelist and poet. His novel *The Vicar of Wakefield* and his play *She Stoops to Conquer* secured his reputation as a novelist and playwright respectively.

5. Buchanan has likened St Andrews Bay, a fairly open stretch of water off the famous golfing and historical town of St Andrews, to the Bay of Biscay, which is particularly notorious for the unpredictable nature of the storms that develop there.

6. At this Journal's time of writing, the Confederate states during the American Civil War were being blockaded by ships of the Union forces. As a consequence they were actively purchasing ships which could outrun the Union vessels.

7. The *Admella* was shipwrecked in a storm off Cape Northumberland on the South Australia coast in 1859. There were only a few survivors, who were rescued only after they had clung to the wreckage for eight days.

8. Buchanan here is referring to his wife, who had died in March 1855.

9. Peterhead is a fishing port a few miles to the north of Aberdeen in north-east Scotland.

10. The River Youghie (or Ugie, the modern spelling), enters the North Sea at the town of Peterhead.

11. Continuations were gaiters or cloth leggings, which were worn by men in continuation with a pair of knee-length breeches.

12. Anabella Buchanan, who was celebrating her 19th birthday.

13. Lines from the Scottish poet Robert Burns's famous work 'Tam o' Shanter'.

14. A French-administered island, in the Indian Ocean, south-west of Australia.

15. Sir John Francis Campbell of Islay, 1822–85, a native of Islay in the western Scottish Hebridean islands. He was educated at Eton and Edinburgh University, and as a Gaelic scholar he held several prestigious offices in the legal and civil service professions. He had several works published about the West Highlands.

16. An expression in the local dialect for falling and landing on the posterior in cattle dung lying on a path or in a field.

17. Matthew Fontaine Maury, 1806–73, a native of Virginia who joined the US navy in 1825. He was appointed superintendent of the hydrographical office in Washington in 1842. He wrote an important work, *Physical Geography of the Sea*, which was published in 1856. He became an officer in the Confederate navy during the American Civil War, and was later Professor of Physics at Lexington University.

18. The *Great Eastern* was built at Blackwall in London, and designed by the great Victorian engineer Isambard Kingdom Brunel.

19. Although considered an offensive expression in the present day, the use of the word 'coolie' by white people to describe native peoples of regions such as south-east Asia was not uncommon and not considered derogatory during the Victorian era.

20. As in the previous note, the expression 'darkie' was another word considered inoffensive when referring to non-white races.

21. Sir James Duke, like Buchanan, was born in Montrose, Angus. During the early to mid 19th century he carved out a career in politics and commerce in England, and was a Lord Mayor of London.

22. Joseph Hume, 1777–1855, was also born in Montrose, Angus, and studied medicine at Edinburgh University. He worked for the East India Company as an assistant surgeon, and later served in Parliament, primarily between 1819 and 1855. He was pro-Reform and argued for the legalisation of trades unions.

23. The *Bellerophon* was a British warship which achieved fame for taking Napoleon Bonaparte to prison exile in St Helena off the West African coast in 1815. The ship ended its days as a prison hulk on the River Thames, near London.

24. Located in the estuary of the River Forth, between the Midlothian and Fife shores, Inchcolm island is the site of a ruined abbey and is sometimes referred to as the Iona of the east of Scotland.

25. James Stuart of Dunearn, 1775–1849. He was born in Dunearn, Fife and in time became a landowner, politician and factory inspector. He studied law at Edinburgh University and was called to the bar in 1798. He was a keen

farmer and a fervent Whig in his politics. He often threatened physical violence to his Tory opponents in the Tory-controlled Edinburgh Town Council. He became involved in several public incidents of violence and more than once challenged individuals to duels. On one occasion he duelled with Alexander Boswell of Auchinleck (the son of James Boswell of Samuel Johnson fame) in Fife in 1822. Boswell died of injuries the following day and Stuart fled to France, but eventually returned to face trial and was acquitted. He was declared bankrupt in 1828, and moved to London where he died in 1849, after having edited the Whig newspaper, the *Courier*, during the 1830s.

26. The Battle of Antietam in 1862 was a crucial conflict between the Unionist and Confederate armies during the American Civil War.

27. James Boswell, Samuel Johnson's biographer and travelling companion.

28. James Boswell's father.

29. Pasquale de Paoli, 1725–1807, a Corsican patriot who became Governor of Corsica after the French Revolution. Dissatisfied with French rule, he masterminded an insurrection, but was forced into exile in England in 1796.

30. Roughly translated: 'What do you think of our James? He was at first friendly with an asylum-seeking scoundrel named Paoli, and now he's in tow with an old teacher, a Doctor Johnson, who ran a school and called it an academy.'

31. Philip Massinger, 1583–1640, an English dramatist whose works included *A New Way to Pay Old Debts*, written in 1633 and generally regarded as a brilliant comedy and satirical study.

32. Tom Sayers, 1826–65, was the English heavyweight boxing champion in 1857. Formerly a bricklayer, he took up boxing in 1849, and lost only one fight in his career. He fought an American, John C. Heenan, for the first world heavyweight championship in April 1860. The fight ended in a draw, after 42 rounds that lasted two hours and six minutes. Remarkably, although a heavyweight, Sayers was only 11 stones in weight.

33. It may be that John C. Heenan was more commonly known as Jack, going by Buchanan's narrative. However, it is fairly certain that the sport of boxing as it was then organised during mid-Victorian times was popular enough to support exhibition bouts in cities such as Glasgow and elsewhere.

34. Prestonpans was a battle during the Jacobite rising of 1745, when Charles Stuart's (the Young Pretender's, or Bonnie Prince Charlie's) forces were victorious and marched south in an attempt to wrest the British crown from the Hanoverian monarchy.

35. Valued in current prices at £36.40 per acre. See note 6 for June 1863.

36. Kilmun developed as a small holiday resort on the Clyde estuary and is situated on a point of land named Strone Point where the waters of the Clyde estuary, the Holy Loch and Loch Long all meet.

37. See August, note 12.

38. Archibald Constable, 1774–1827. Born in Fife, he started as a bookseller in 1795, became a publisher and counted Sir Walter Scott among his authors. He bought the *Scots Magazine* in 1801 and launched the soon to be influential *Edinburgh Review* in 1802. He was declared bankrupt in 1826.

39. Maria Edgeworth, 1767–1849, Irish novelist and the daughter of an inventor and educationist, Richard Lovell Edgeworth, 1744–1817. Educated in England, she returned to Ireland to work as her father's assistant and he greatly influenced her literary career. She was particularly admired for her children's stories.

40. The press was a system that the Royal Navy used to maintain the manpower for its warships, particularly during times of war, or when there was a need to provide a naval presence in various parts of the world. Selected officers and seamen would patrol ports and inshore waters, and would literally seize individuals and have them taken aboard a warship where they would serve until it returned to port or hostilities ceased. Among the lower classes of British society few males were exempt.

41. John Clerk, Lord Eldin, 1757–1832. He studied law, and soon made his mark at the Scottish Bar. He eventually acquired an extensive legal practice. In politics he was a keen Whig, and in the late 18th century contributed notably to the movement for burgh reform. He was appointed a Law Lord in 1823, assuming the title of Lord Eldin. His time as a judge was not considered a success. Over his lifetime he had amassed a vast collection of paintings and prints, and after his death in 1832 the collection was put up for auction. It is claimed that the sale had to be spread over 14 days, due to the sheer size of the collection.

42. Lord Hermand (George Ferguson), 1743–1827, was born in Ayrshire, studied law at Edinburgh University and pursued a legal career, becoming a member of the Faculty of Advocates in 1765. He was elevated to the Court of Session in 1799 as Lord Hermand. He took his judicial title from his country estate of Hermand at West Calder,

a village to the west of Edinburgh. He married late, in 1893, to a daughter of William MacDowall, a merchant, of Garthland in Galloway, having no children. He had a legendary capacity for drink, and it was said that he could imbibe leaving others on the floor drunk and unconscious, after several hours of consuming hard liquor. He was always clear-eyed at his court the following day, when as often as not his drinking companions of the previous day were absent.

43. The Scottish poet Robert Burns, 1759–96. Famous internationally, particularly for the traditional New Year lyrics of the song 'Auld Lang Syne'.

44. A mollyhawk or mollymawk is a seabird that is a smaller kind of albatross.

October 1863

1 October, 9 a.m. – 'Land! Land!' was the cry along the deck. I was rather sceptical at first, but on looking more narrowly, I could trace with the naked eye, better than with the glass, the dark outline of a land stretching along, somewhat like the ridge of the Campsie hills,[1] although what was now dimly seen on our starboard bow must have been a mountainous region, otherwise it would not have loomed forth at such a distance.

We concluded that it was Banks' Peninsula, in the province of Christchurch, in New Zealand's South Island, and so named after that Sir Joseph [Banks] who accompanied Captain Cook on his second voyage.

And was this the land that was discovered by James Cook[2] and which now I gaze upon? The land which my boyish fancy associated with sunny skies, crystal streams, and verdant shade.

I felt a strange sensation, a busy something within me. A belief that I had been rather destined to accompany Cook, to whose course we have on the whole closely adhered, as Cook was indeed a splendid navigator. Instead of my being in a passenger ship, I would have been prepared, on setting foot on land, to find the forms, modes, and shores of the older country. I should like to have seen the tattooed warriors sailing forth in their canoes from the Waitangi, the mouth of which stream we must have passed the other day.

When we left England the Maoris, by the last accounts, had not abandoned their hostile attitude – and who among us can tell what they may be now doing! – but they now employ a different species of warlike weapons, for their lances and clubs have now evolved into muskets, which they can handle with barbarian precision.

The ship was in a state of excitement today. People would not settle down as they were generally accustomed to do. A cry was raised a little time ago, 'A seal, a seal, on the port beam!' I thought the voice announced, 'A sail, a sail!' and I was disappointed to find that it was nothing of the sort, but was, however, a sign of land. I have frequently seen seals disporting on the Drumly Sands, where the Tay[3] debouches into the German

Ocean – a coast whereon if a ship stranded in an easterly gale there was no hope of life to the mariner, except by holding on by the rigging.

By 12 o'clock, noon we had let down 70 fathoms of line, but not touched the bottom. There was not a breath of wind stirring, and the sea was beautifully calm to the eye; but the water no longer possessed that blue aspect to which we were accustomed in the tropical latitudes – it was now of a dark greenish hue.

At three o'clock a little wind came, and light staysails were hoisted. I was laughed at by some last Saturday because I took a bet that the anchor would not be let go at or before 12 o'clock on Saturday next. They calculated that the ship would continue, as previously, to go over 5 or 6 degrees of longitude in the 24 hours, whereas I concluded that, as we neared the land, we could no longer reckon upon the duration of either a strong or a steady and favourable wind.

A sailing vessel may run from Boston or Halifax to the Chops of the English Channel in 18 or 16 days, but it may take as many more before it rounds the South Foreland and gets into the Downs.

Accordingly, it is now in the dice that I should not be the loser. A ship nearing land is not like a coach or railway train approaching its destination. We may be a few days or upwards of a week before we reach Auckland, but it cannot be before Saturday at noon.

A good deal of speculation was also going on as to the pending sweepstakes. Some are hedging and some are betting on the probable winner, as those at home are wont to do upon the Derby and St. Leger. We have already have two among us who are done for. Fred Paul went out of contention today, and Mr. Welby, M.R.C.S., London, at the same hour yesterday. I hold the chance from 12 noon on Thursday next, the 8th of October, until the same hour on Friday. Nalder follows me, and then comes Johnnie Hanson.

We three last mentioned have coalesced, but I have inserted a special clause that little Jonas Willan shall receive a crown out of the stakes, if we are successful. We thought that by thus enlarging our net we might catch the prize. But I ought to remember that a coalition seldom prospers. It is a word of evil omen in English constitutional history, and so it ought to be, for it implies awkward elements thrown together, with no clarity of agreement, and little vigour for unity of action.

By eight o'clock in the evening the wind had freshened a little from an hour previously, and we were making 7 knots, but were about two points off our course. What is more, our vicinity to the land rendered it prudent to brace more sharply than we would otherwise have done, and thus lose the full advantage of such wind as we had.

At 9.30 in the evening the order was given, 'All hands up – about ship,' and the captain told me that a similar order would probably be given at four o'clock tomorrow morning, when the watch was shifted; in other words, the wind was against us, and we had to keep tacking.

Latitude 44° 26' S., longitude 174° 48' E.

2 October – A beautiful clear morning, with a stiff but a foul wind, for it blew sharp on our starboard bows, and compelled us to be close hauled. At ten o'clock a.m. we were putting ship about, and in short, kept knocking off and on the shore, as we did when we were beating down the English Channel – one moment fetching the coast of France, and then sighting the cliffs of Albion.

There was no land in view today, and it would not have been so desirable if there was. He cared not much for land or soundings, did our captain, for there were such repulsive objects as rocks and coral reefs amidst the subtle crannies of the deep, not to speak of leeshore perils which we knew nothing of, when we were bounding over its mighty caverns, during hundreds of miles of offing.

Yesterday, as I have already stated, the ship, or rather its occupants, were in considerable excitement. I found my little friend, Jonas Willan, with his broad shoulders on a level with the taffrail, and his feet resting on the sheet of the spanker boom. Methinks, Jonas, this was no place for thee, as a lurch on that rope could easily send thee and thrice thy weight heels up overboard.

I remonstrated with Jonas, but he deemed himself insulted, thinking that I was questioning his courage, and he stoutly refused to take my counsel and come off.

However, it was necessary to take active measures with Jonas, seeing that he gave no heed to my advice. I pulled out a strap, and before Jonas could say John Robinson, Esquire, I had him firmly by the ankle, and the other end of the strap made fast to the braces. How fiercely Jonas did kick and vainly struggle, until at length our parson, Mr. Lopdell, came, like the good Samaritan, to his liberation.

At eight o'clock in the evening I was writing that, earlier, while on making the port tack, we had come, at one o'clock in the afternoon, within view of the land, and a range of mountains, one or two of which were capped with snow. What a splendid sight! I have had more or less exciting moments in my existence, as most men have had. I knew nothing that has surpassed the sight of those mountains. I admit, that, in some measure, distance leads enchantment to the view. However, I did feel such a glow of excitement rush through my veins.

The decks were crowded with an eager throng. But it was time to put about, and we soon bore off the land. The wind blew strongly, and, being on our bows, we did pitch at a lively rate, but the passengers could bear it better than rolling, although it ministered not to our progress. We again came in sight of land between six and seven o'clock earlier in the evening, and that necessitated shorter tacks.

Latitude 43° 11' S., longitude 175° 0' E., or about 90 miles off the River Hurunui, in the province of Nelson, South Island. Temperature 58F.

3 October – The wind continued adverse, and there was nothing for it but tacking. We saw the land about half past eight this morning, and now, at half past eleven, we were again in sight of lofty mountains.

The land seen yesterday must have been upwards of 9,000 feet high, or three times the height of Ben Lomond.[4] The mountainous ridge which we viewed today attained an elevation of 9,700 feet, and was nine miles from the coast. There may have been a good strip of land which intervened in that portion of the South Island, but I suspected there was a better soil inland, or behind those mountains.

The summits were covered with perpetual snow, and I could distinctly trace with the naked eye the white and extensive stripes of freestone or limestone, running down the slopes, which may betoken a country which possessed valuable minerals. The white man would eventually have it all, and the black man would go to the wall. Such, under Providence, was the appointed order of affairs.

I saw our sailors polishing away at our oars, that we may row ashore in befitting style. There were two blades which attracted my admiration, for they were so slim and beautifully formed. I defy even the marine establishments of Scotland to surpass those fins.

At eight o'clock in the evening the wind had become a shade more favourable, and we were making something of it, although still closely hauled. At twelve o'clock noon, earlier today I had to punish my Gloucester agricultural friend. Last week, at the like hour, I was engaged in the same painful duty. I offered him another bet, but he thought he had already had enough of the Scotch thistle.

I recollected a fine specimen of that emblem of Scotia which figured in a procession on the banks of Doon,[5] when a festival took place in honour of Robert Burns. I should have liked to have once more gazed on the well where 'Mungo's mither hang'd hersel', and the brig across which Tam o' Shanter took his flight on that eventful night, the more especially as one of the best and truest young friends I ever met does dwell and prosper on the banks of Ayr. His last words to me on parting were that we two had been linked in sorrow.

But I have this day looked upon other scenes. We must now be approaching Cook's Straits, and going more in our course. I hope we will not have to put about the ship again this night. We could now run to Auckland in three days if we had a fair wind and enough of it. As we have sighted the land, I need not repeat the latitude and longitude.

4 October, Sunday – I walked along the main deck in the morning at six o'clock, when very few, excepting the watch, were astir. We were approaching Cook's Straits, and sighted an apparently low ridge of hills on our port quarter, but very different from the stupendous heights we had looked upon yesterday and the preceding day.

This proved to be the northern part of the island of New Zealand that we were coasting along. The wind had got abaft, and was favourable, but scarcely a puff to fill the cloud of duck that we had spread.

I walked up to the poop, where I found Captain Funnell and Mr. Woolley busily scanning the compass, to ascertain, as I presumed, the variation. I told them that they need not be so anxious, as only a few minutes previously I had learned that there was a man from the West of Scotland down below, who knew more about the matter than either of them, or the illustrious Captain James Cook to boot.

That west-land navigator had received the cognomen of Captain from some of the Englishmen around him. Pope, the philosopher of poets, to whom Wordsworth could not hold the lamp, said truly, 'But fools rush in where angels fear to tread.' I may, in reference to that observation, be impeached for heresy by the admirers of the Lakeish school.

At 11 o'clock in the forenoon the wind got right abaft, and we flew along at from 10 to 11 knots, with royals and all other square sails set. In the course of the forenoon we came in sight of the land of the North or Middle Island. The hills were distinctly seen, and also a promontory which we put down as Cape Palliser, with Cook's Straits stretching away to the westward.

Later in the afternoon, at five o'clock, a sudden and fierce squall or gale came from the south westward, and blew loud and strong, as it still does. All hands were called, and no time was lost in taking in sail. Eventually we were only carrying one reefed topsail on the main and the like on the foremast, with foresail and foretop staysail.

We had a pelting rain, the dead-lights were clapped on to the skylights, and the captain looks forward to a dirty night. A sail was seen in the distance this morning, but it soon disappeared. It looked as if bound for Cook's Straits.

5 October, Monday – A little after eight o'clock last night the wind, which had been blowing stiffly since five o'clock, quickened into a regular hard gale, and came off in fierce gusts, which rendered it impossible to keep the deck without holding on. What a roar the tempest had, but the *Ganges* behaved beautifully. It was a rough night, and the gale was carrying us along at 12 knots.

At six o'clock in the morning I walked up to the quarter deck, where I found the captain and Mr. Valentine, the second officer. As for the captain, poor man, I don't know when he managed to rest, for he had been up for the last two nights. The vicinity of land, of course, rendered him anxious.

As I was standing talking a roll came, and I was forced to lay hold of the hencoop. I judged it prudent to take myself to the main deck, for it was rather sheltered from the gale, which came over the starboard quarter, or very nearly abaft, and loudly and roughly it did blow. I saw one sea fly over the starboard beam, which drenched three or four who were in its way, and set the water a-swimming on the main deck.

We had no sail set save the lower top on the main, and the foresail, foretop staysail, and lower top on the foremast, or four sails in all. But the gale was on the decline, as, at seven o'clock in the morning, I heard the order given to let down the mizzentopsail, and in half an hour afterwards the cross-jack was let go. The sun was shining brightly, and the rate from eleven to twelve knots.

At 12 o'clock, noon, we had once more what we considered comparatively quiet weather, with the land in sight on the port bow. We concluded that we were nigh to Hawke Bay. Last night the ocean, while lashed by the gale, assumed a brilliant phosphoric aspect. When the gale came rushing out of the south yesterday, Mr. Green, who happened to be near the man at the wheel, flew to his aid, and his powerful arms did good service.

At four o'clock p.m. we shortened sail, in order that we would not near the East Cape before four o'clock tomorrow morning, or with daylight.

The captain was joking me today about accompanying him to Calcutta as supercargo, as I seemed to take so kindly with the sea. I said I would readily go there, or round the other half of the world, with him and his good ship, provided only I had my belongings comfortably disposed, for that was the primary consideration. There were many comforts at sea, and, among others, as Tom Sutton remarks, one was not bothered with income-tax or church and poor-rates.

In the evening the ship rolled heavily, as the wind had gone nearly aft.

6 October, Tuesday – After a storm comes a calm. On Sunday evening and yesterday morning it blew great guns, quite a southern burster, as Jack colloquially termed it. Today was deliciously soft, the air delightful to inhale and the ocean was like a mill pond, figuratively speaking, and all on board were in jolly good humour.

Did I say all? May I be pardoned the expression, as our good and gallant captain was an exception. Not that he was in bad humour – far be it from me to say so – for at that moment he passed the sofa on which I am seated, exchanged a word with me, and declared that we must surely have some Jonah on board.

I promised to him either to whistle for a breeze, and throw the Jonah overboard, once he is found, or if he would allow me one of our pinnaces, and also the second officer, Old Chips the carpenter, with three Jacks, including Le Maire, our Jersey man, I would push off for Auckland and announce to the agents, and all whom it may concern, that the *Ganges* is a 'comin'', as little Jonas would say.

Captain Funnell graciously accepted my first proposition, but he courteously, though firmly, declined the latter or alternative issue, as he neither wished to part with me, nor, with what is of far more importance, his pinnace and her proposed crew.

Nevertheless, give us an ample supply of water, and five or six days grog, and, barring another southern burster, I think we could manage it within two days or less, if we plied our oars steadily and handily when our sails failed us.

I have referred to Le Maire; he is a tight-built, comely young sailor, and, what was better still, he had this day offered to cleanse a pair of my continuations, which, in a gale, shipped a plate of pease soup. He wears rings in his ears, and altogether he is a very proper young man, to my taste.

The speculation as to the sweepstakes became more keener as the chances narrowed. The doctor and Fred Paul were respectively thrown out on the first and second day after the log was hove and the glass began to run. Tom Sutton, to my sorrow, followed suit on the third day; Mr. Charles Paul vanished on the Sunday; Captain Marshall departed life on the Monday, and Mr. Stopford lapsed today, when Mr. Woolley commenced to run the race at 12 o'clock noon, and he will be distanced tomorrow at the same hour. Then Mr. Vaughan goes in, and, if the anchor is not down by 12 o'clock noon on Thursday, I and Nalder and Johnnie Hanson will most likely jointly catch the whale, as we have the game in our own hands for three days, or 72 hours.

It was said by some of the forward passengers that land was seen at five o'clock this morning. Mr. Woolley ascended to the mast-head about that hour, but he could not say that he distinctly made out the said land. However, we have people on board, and from Scotland, who professed to see much farther than our captain and his officers.

They saw what was had from the lynx eyes of Thomas Woolley, and they also currently reported that the light on East Cape had been visible to the swarthy cook (not the great navigator) at two o'clock this morning, when the officer on the watch had flashed a light to inform the lighthouse-keeper that a sail was passing.

Now it happened that there was no lighthouse on the promontory I have named, and that the light actually flashed was directed to some object supposed to be a vessel. Had there existed a light, and we had sighted it, then the captain could have taken his bearings from it, and so far, abridged our course.

The wind has been on our port bows, or all but ahead, and the ship was consequently very closely hauled. At three o'clock in the afternoon we put about in the direction of the land or on the port tack.

At a little before six o'clock in the evening the East Cape was distinctly sighted, with two large and three smaller hummocks; and at seven o'clock the ship was put on the opposite tack, for we cared not much for the company of the land when the darkness overtakes us. The sea was quite smooth this evening, and it was quite easy to write in the saloon.

I saw the poor Canadian sailor, to whom I formerly referred, sitting under the forecastle today, and looking miserably ill. I conversed with him, when he told me that he was worse, and thought that the cold had settled down on his lungs, adding, 'I fear, sir, that I'm in a bad way.' I tried to cheer him with the hope of recuperating when he got ashore at Auckland. I think he will rally under that care which one cannot expect to be practicable on board of ship.

Temperature 65F. Today had afforded a very favourable opinion of the New Zealand home in the North Island.

7 October, Wednesday – Another balmy and lovely day, with little or no wind. The ship moved and no more. I walked up to the poop between four and five this morning and viewed the sunrise. It was magnificent. As I could not find my cap at the time, I clapped on an ordinary but perfectly good hat, hailing from Gardiner's,[6] Bell Street, Glasgow.

Wearing that strange apparel I was spotted from the cook's galley and in the course of the morning it was reported through the forward part of the ship that the pilot had come aboard, as he had been seen on the poop, arrayed in a sort of guise that evidently smelt of the shore, and eagerly conferred with the captain and Mr. Valentine, the second officer.

Idle people, and at sea, will live their joke, and all quite right. I will never part with that hat, because it was purchased for me by two most kind friends on the night I departed Scotland, and was about to go aboard the night train for England.

I will further cling to it, because it has been (unknown to me) encircled by the cunning hand of my Sally with a crimson stripe, and an anchor, worked in front. It shall, therefore, be retained by me as a memory of the present voyage.

At five o'clock I joined the captain and Valentine in the usual cup of tea or coffee which is at that hour of the morning carried into the quarter deck. In the forenoon the atmosphere was so clear and delightful that few or none were disposed to sit down and read or go about any light work.

Some of the ladies, however, had got a portion of their boxes out of the hold, and seemed very agreeably employed in donning their handsome neat bonnets, which had not been seen by their bright eyes for months, and then admired their fair countenances as reflected in the mirror.

The gentlemen took the liberty of offering a few, and, of course, flattering, criticisms. All were out on deck except one or two invalids. The Canadian sailor, to whom I referred yesterday, was looking better today. He told me that he expected, if he got a few days in the hospital at Auckland, to be able to accompany the *Ganges* to Calcutta.

There is one most amiable and intelligent young man in the second cabin, to whom this charming weather, I fear, brings no relief. He had good hopes, as we were coming out of the tropics, and getting into a more temperate clime, for he had suffered from the heat. But he was again shaken by the cold weather and gales which we encountered when rounding the Cape. I have not seen him out on the deck since the last and stormy Sunday and Monday, which he was ill fitted to stand. I have observed that the strong, wiry, sinewy frame is best calculated to endure heat or cold.

I had a relative who, after serving four years in the Indian, Borneo, and China Seas, in the *Agincourt*, 72 guns, and *Spiteful*, 6 guns (a steam-flapper), volunteered (for that choice lot of ocean chivalry were all volunteers) as one of the officers of H.M. discovery ship *Investigator*, which, along with the *Enterprise*, was sent in search of Franklin.[7] Another very good friend of mine was the master on board the *Enterprise*.

These two vessels passed one winter in Prince Regent's Inlet. On their return, after 18 months absence from England, they were, within six weeks, again put in commission to go in quest of Franklin, but in the opposite direction, or round Cape Horn to the Pacific, and up Bering's Straits, and along the north-west coast of America.

My friend, as he again volunteered, and accompanied that expedition, passed nigh to one extremity of the vast American continent on the 14th April, 1849, and passed the other, or southern extremity, on the same day in 1850, or in twelve months.

It did not return until five years and four months had elapsed since it had sailed from England. Three of those years were passed amidst the ice, cut off from all intercourse with the civilised world.

After undergoing the inevitable hardships of that voyage, and passing round the world, it was my sad lot to lay my relative's head in the grave, close by the side of one very near and still more dear to us both.[8]

The sea was still calm, and scarcely any wind stirred. What a sky! The dark blue, the red, and the azure coming resplendently forth as the sun went down. There was considerable excitement on board at the thought of reaching Auckland. In the present state of the weather, there was little hope of that event tomorrow, or the day after that. Temperature, 65F.

8 October, Thursday – As I was springing over the lee board of my berth this morning, I heard the boatswain, Lee, who was standing near my port, say something about the tack of the gallant stunsails. A light and fair wind, thought I, and every effort made to draw it to the last inch.

When I ascended the quarter deck I found that such was the state of affairs. I also met Captain Marshall and our own captain pacing the deck with military precision, and with that decisive tread which denoted purpose and resolve in a man.

On the subject of purpose and resolve, the eyes are said to be indicators of the inner self, although I would deem them sometimes both fitful and dangerous signals. I may add that I considered the mouth or the lips to be about as sure, and, in some respects, equally perilous, monitors of the inner self, as too are the eyes.

Macaulay[9] had written of that great man Warren Hastings[10] that he saved to Britain her Indian Empire, as Clive, another of those bright stars who have arisen on our Eastern horizon, had previously done.

Well, of Warren Hastings, and referring to his picture – which, for all I know, now that I have got free and on the run, I may yet see hanging, as it does, in the Town Hall of Calcutta – Macaulay says, 'the mouth indicated inflexible firmness and decision'.

By the way, I have on many an occasion admired the mouth of Macaulay himself, as he stood before the modern Athenians, or electors of Edinburgh, soliciting their sweet voices. I might have shaken his hand one day as he walked forward, in the Waterloo Room, to give his supporters a general and promiscuous hug.

If Macaulay had a finely expressive mouth, he had not otherwise a dignified form; some in Edinburgh, when wincing under the wisdom and eloquence of Macaulay, resorted to the rather pitiful and personal retort of terming him splay-footed Tom. Pray excuse me for this digression, as reminiscences of the past will come on us when coasting along New Zealand, and far away from the old country.

In the course of the forenoon a light wind carried us onward at about four knots; but at five o'clock in the afternoon it had freshened, and gave about nine knots. Land was seen in the morning, which I believe was the northern extremity of what Captain

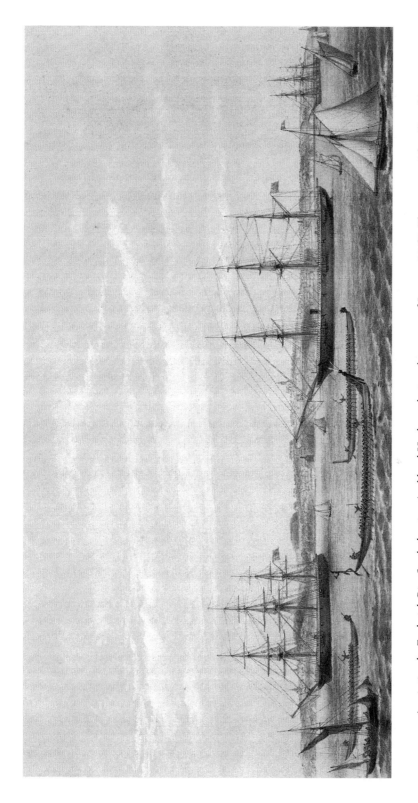

A painting by Frederick Rice Stack showing Auckland Harbour during the regatta of January 1862. The scene – with sailing ships moored in the harbour – would have been similar to that which greeted the Buchanan family and their fellow passengers when the Ganges, sails furled, moored there in October 1863. Courtesy of the Alexander Turnbull Library, Wellington, New Zealand

Cook named the Bay of Plenty. A day or two since we passed the Bay of Poverty, and we trust that we are well past it, for Cook must have experienced a cold reception there.

At eight o'clock in the evening I had calculated that we were not far off the Barrier Island; but I would not ask any questions on the matter, as I could see that the captain was keeping close to the deck, and, no doubt, had his share of anxiety, as all good commanders have when they near the land after a long voyage.

A subscription had been made among the passengers, cabin and forward, to procure some tribute to him and his lady, in token of the gratitude we all owe to him for the manner in which he has handled his ship, and his attention to all on board.

I may say that some few forward – too many Scotsmen included – declined to contribute, but at the same time wished some verbal expression of their good feeling to the captain to be added to the brief address which preceded the subscription list. I strongly advised the party who drew out that address to decline any such proposition.

It reminded me of a story which I once heard delivered with great gusto. A lady, who had taken some umbrage at her parson, showed her injured feelings when she entered the church vestibule, by making a low and formal curtsey to the plate or salver usually placed there to receive the offering to the poor. The beadle (verger) tartly observed, 'Give us less of your manners and more of your money, my lady.'

Temperature, 65F.

9 October, Friday. – Last night there were preparations made for landing at Auckland in the course of today. Some passengers were talking so confidently of the said land, that I was wearied of the very term, and I asked, 'When you get it what will you do with it?' that being something near the title of one of the finest works of that most profound and classical of all our novelists, Sir Edward Lytton Bulwer.[11] He was once a Lord Rector of Glasgow University – one of a galaxy of masters of learning.

A little after four o'clock this morning, when it was dark, I walked along the main deck, where Mr. Woolley twigged my ear before I could do the same to him. The ship was rolling and the wind was blowing, but nothing to trouble those who have been so long on the water. At five o'clock, however, there did come off not a southern burster, but a strong gale, and what was worse, we had a lee shore.

When we were assembled for breakfast at half past eight o'clock, down came Captain Funnell, and tossed his light cap into his chair, replacing it with a south-wester, and ordered the steward to bring his breakfast up to the quarter deck. Still there was no use, come what may, that we should lose a comfortable breakfast – I had to take the chair and serve out the curry – a duty I had to fulfil on a previous occasion, when the captain could not leave the deck to preside at dinner, because the crew were engaged in taking in sail during a squall.

At nine o'clock, Oh! horrible, most horrible! what did we see but an ugly, high, rocky, bluffy island on our lee, while the wind was blowing hard, the atmosphere thick, and the sea tumbling roughly. I saw the captain, with his trusty lieutenants, Woolley and Valentine, like a triumvirate in close discussion on the quarter deck. I did not disturb their serious meditation.

We were close hauled, and had to sail with some risk in the best direction we could, not knowing what might next emerge on our bows, for I heard that some islands were scattered about the locality.

Captain Marshall and I quietly conferred and shook our heads, and we went into the cabin among the ladies, whom I was glad to see sitting quietly at their work, while little Jonas Willan, with a hold of one of the skid poles, was dancing gaily on the main sheet rope.

When I was writing at 12 o'clock, noon, and only two hours or thereby after that critical period, the weather had moderated; but I suspected that the wind was sending us elsewhere than direct to Auckland, in which place some, with rash forethought, had made up their mind to sleep this night. May we be safely cradled on the deep, with plenty of sea room either to tack or wear.

By eight o'clock in the evening it had been raining nearly the whole day with a hazy atmosphere. It descended in torrents, which I hope will prove to be the harbinger of clearer weather. The wind had fallen off, and the old lady rolled heavily.

I was informed by someone earlier that many passengers had lost their sleep last night, and were endeavouring to make up their quota during the course of the day. I do not think that I have deemed our situation this day more hazardous than it really was; for the truth is, that I have made no inquiries as to our position or anything else. It was, however, sufficiently apparent that the captain and officers were fully occupied with their own thoughts, and I know well that the captain will not seek his berth tonight. We concluded however that we must be near Mercury Island.

The other day we were talking of different cities, and I ascertained that only one of our cabin friends – viz., Mr. Charles Paul, of Bristol – had visited Edinburgh. I produced some photographic views of Sir Walter Scott's own romantic town, which were very much admired.

These, which are admirably executed, were presented to me by a kind friend in Glasgow, whom I liked at first sight. I have never forgot the pleasant dinner party we had on the day of our introduction, when his brother, who occupied an honourable position in our mercantile marine service, formed one of the company.

10 October – Saturday, and all's well that ends well, although we cannot say that we were as yet done with it, for at 10.30 a.m. I heard the order, 'About ship', or 'All hands on deck', which told me that we must tack.

The night had, no doubt, been an anxious one to our able captain, because a ship nigh to an iron-bound coast, with currents running and little wind blowing, is not an enviable state of matters even at the best, if any best there can be in these circumstances. Fortunately, however, at five o'clock the daylight came, and the atmosphere cleared.

I walked along the deck a little after six in the morning, when a magnificent spectacle greeted and gladdened the eye as we were coasting along the Great Barrier Island.

I have seen a fair share of Scotland and of her Highland scenery, both inland and coastwise, but I do not think, so far as my observation has gone – for I never visited Staffa and Iona[12] – that anything in my travels had rivalled the scenery which was now on our port side.

A good way astern was a promontory, with a huge isolated rock standing out from it. It much more resembled Ailsa Craig[13] than it did the Bass Rock;[14] indeed, I could have almost imagined that the former had been transplanted, and stood before me in the Southern Sea.

I referred to a rock like Ailsa Craig on the south, but to the northward we were close upon the Aguilles, or Needles Point, a series of pyramids or obelisks springing out of the ocean. Away to the north-eastward we descried the Island of Motohinoa, and also the isles called the Little Barriers.

As the day drew on, we found our ship amidst small, bold, rocky isles, one of these surpassing in its lofty, serrated, and eccentric ridge even the peaks called the Cobbler, as seen when sailing up the beautiful waters of Loch Long and Loch Goil;[15] where we also view Ben Una, which is translated the rich in verdure, while Ben Thiola signifies in the Gaelic, abounding in springs and water cresses; and another mountain situated there, Ben Luibhan, means profuse of herbs.

We could make out some herbage on the rocky inlets, among which we were tacking about today, and I daresay our captain in his heart's core wished that we were well free of such dangerous neighbours.

We had been contending throughout the day with a head wind, which blew rather stiff at five in the afternoon. Our endeavour had been to beat so far to windward as to enable us to weather the northern point of the Great Barrier Island, and get into the long bay, at the head of which is situated the capital, Auckland, near to a stream called after Old Father Thames. Smoke was seen rising from the shore, and some brushwood was burning, and at night the Needles, which we had seen in the morning, were distinctly visible astern.

It was a weary and anxious worry for our captain and officers. At eight o'clock in the evening I heard the order to take in the foretopgallant, that we may go under easy sail during the night. The sea was smooth, which rendered it easy to read or write, as compared with the nights when we were in the South Atlantic, or amidst some of the teasers which we had since experienced in the Indian and South Seas.

I was agreeably interrupted by Tom Sutton entering the cabin with a beam of hilarity on his face, and taking one or two lively skips as he sang, 'Music has charms to soothe the savage breast, but doesn't enable us to pay the income tax.' Tom also considers this a 'deuced healthy place which will make a fellow eat'.

Another Saturday night overtook us, being the sixteenth which we have passed at sea. I believe that we are about 20 miles from any prudent or practical anchorage ground.

Our sweepstakes had terminated in smoke, as Johnnie Hanson, the last of the lot, would pass the deadline tomorrow at 12 o'clock, when there was as little chance of our anchor being down off Auckland as off Dumbarton Castle. The result will be that in the evening, or on the first lawful day, there will be another draw for the swag, to use the classic language of those minions of the moon – Dick Turpin, Captain Macheath, Jack Sheppard, and last, but not least, David Haggart,[16] of Scottish, and especially Dumfriesian, notoriety.

David Haggart was quite worthy to stand forth as the representative of Scotland in the light-fingered school. I saw him on the day before George IV was crowned, step forth on the scaffold, when the hangman's rope effectually finished him, although I ran off to the Edinburgh High School – where I was past due – not desiring to witness his fall and final consummation. It was too much for my boyish tender nature.

They have this evening again drawn for the sweepstakes, but as I do not care for that sort of thing, although I did not wish to offend my young friends when it was started, I thought it now high time to withdraw. My crown was accordingly restored to me, but I requested it be presented to John Harris, a fine, ingenuous-looking youth of 18 from the Isle of Man, without friends and without money, as my boy told me that he was expecting to land without sixpence in his pocket.

I am sorry to say that the poor young man to whom I alluded as being in a hopeless state was very low today. It was even doubtful if he would ever land.

11 October – *Soonday*, as little Jonas Willan would say, and he never failed to remember the importance of that day, for on it there was a dessert in the cabin, and he always received a portion of my share, or his noots as he called it.

This was a lovely morning, as I saw and felt when I looked out of my port at five o'clock. I lost no time in being upon deck, and found that we were running right into the channel under a nice breeze.

I noticed there an honest countrywoman, as she proved to be, who liked her pipe. Having by chance a pipe in my pocket, which had been skilfully loaded by my good friend Woolley, our first officer, I courteously presented it to her, and it was graciously accepted. She told me that she came from that fine part of Scotland called Dumfriesshire, where lie the ashes of Robert Burns.

But my newly found friend had scarcely got her pipe lit and well under way when she commenced to upbraid me, not angrily, but seriously and lovingly, as to why I had spoken to this one and the other around her and had failed to greet her until we were about to wind-up our long voyage.

I made my apology in the best manner I could, by telling her that it had been my unlucky fate never to have discovered her vices or her virtues until the eleventh hour, adding that it was better late than never. She was mollified, and told me that she had enjoyed an excellent pipe.

Mr. Welby, our surgeon, told me that many on board are now complaining, which I suppose is mainly caused by a vibrant impatience for the land, and that desire promises soon to be gratified. Needless to say, the ship is in a state of great excitement today.

Our good cabin parson, Clopdell, was going to officiate, and had the harmonium brought out, and was about to get it rigged up in the saloon by the side of the mizzen. I quietly told him that there was a time for everything, which he ought to know better than me, and that the cabin was in no humour or proper frame for the Church of England any more than the forward passengers were for the Church of Scotland service. The latter, I understand, was very thinly attended.

I proceeded to make a round of farewell visits. In the first place I paid my respects to my honest, hard working, and most ingenious friend, Chips the carpenter, whose cabin was situated under the forecastle on the port side, in which he and Edward Lowe, the young apprentice, are berthed. I had a bottle of ale for him in my pocket, and as there was no screw at hand, Chips got a knife, with which he gave the neck of the bottle three or four most mystical knocks, when out flew the cork, and in flew the beer into a pannikin.

He told me that he was seriously thinking of eventually settling in New Zealand, for he could erect houses as well as ships. I replied that I thought it would be a very judicious step for one of his skill and physical ability. I also reminded him that he should be less sparing of his robust language, for, to say the least, it was a very bad habit, adding that I was aware it did not arise out of any bad disposition, or a desire to harm his fellow creatures. The tall, honest Prussian eyed me steadily, shook his head and said, 'O no, no, sir; you well kno's that.'

My opinion is that one like John Wesley,[17] who once held forth on a beautiful spot near Carmyle,[18] on the Clyde, was much better calculated to find fault with such a vice than the ordinary run of Scotch parson.

After bidding adieu to Chips, I called on Master Lee, our trusty boatswain, who holds out in a plain but tidy cabin on the starboard of the forecastle. Besides being a fine sailor, I found him also an intelligent man, who entertained what I deemed a few shrewd ideas on colonial policy.

Parting with him, I, in the course of the afternoon, called upon, Sails, as our sailmaker was familiarly termed, who was berthed along with Mr. Dobbin, an apprentice of the better class, and two of the stewards, in a cabin in the round or deck-house right abaft the cook's galley. He was also very skilful in his vocation, and a sober, intelligent man. His name was Benjamin Forbes, and he told me that although he was an Englishman his family on the father's side originally hailed from Aberdeenshire.

Our captain, in the course of the forenoon, turned in to snatch a little hard earned rest, for he had been 36 hours on the deck. I trusted that he would have a proper spell of it to-morrow night, with our anchor let go in good holding ground.

At one o'clock p.m. we had been coasting near the land, and spotted several small craft – schooners, cutters, and the native rig. One schooner especially, with her white sails set, came into beautiful relief. The ship was all agog with excitement as we saw clearings and two dwellings – a strange sight to us, who have gazed on nothing save each other and the world of water for nearly four months.

At eight o'clock in the evening the ship was lying to, with the respective lights on port and starboard bows, to prevent collision with any of the small craft that may be cruising about. We had flashed a light, and think we saw it answered from the shore.

How still all seemed tonight. We might suppose ourselves sitting in the Royal Exchange[19] of Glasgow, so steady was the ship after the motion to which we had been long accustomed. The stars shone out, and altogether it was a brilliant night. We expect that the pilot has sighted our light, and will be aboard in the course of the morning.

12 October, Monday – A beautiful day it was, and an exciting one it would prove to be for us all, for some of us will land, although we would return in the evening to sleep on board the ship. On either side of us we saw rocks and dales – the scene very picturesque. Only those who have been over one hundred and ten days afloat can tell the sensation that overcame the many on board the *Ganges*.

Alas! there was one melancholy exception to the general feeling. As I passed along the main deck in a happy mood I came opposite to the cabin of poor young Crawford, which opened on to the deck from the roundhouse, and saw his brother and Mr. Welby, the surgeon in anxious consultation. My eye caught the blanket and coverlet at the foot of the couch whereon lay stretched the ailing form, from which life was fast ebbing away. He was to be conveyed ashore that evening; but it would only be to die, and very soon at that.

I saw Le Maire lashed to the shrouds and heaving the lead, which nearly strikes the head of a gaping fool, who would look over the ship's side. The British ensign was up, and the pilot smack or cutter was seen rapidly approaching us. Two figures dropped into her dinghy, which pulled for our lee side. In a tinkling the pilot ascended, sprang over the gangway, and stood beside our captain on the quarter deck at ten o'clock a.m.

All fell back from the two, who, after a shake of the hand, proceed to confer as if they had known each other for ten years, instead of having met for the first time in their lives. Mr. Pilot Burgess, who was a wiry, genteel-built man, then took command of the *Ganges*, and promptly gave forth his orders. Apart from those aboard the ship, his was the first voice we had heard since a Deal boatman boarded us on 24th June last.

In a few minutes afterwards, as I was sitting in the saloon, down came our own good Captain Funnell, now honourably released from his toils and anxieties. He had a bundle of newspapers in his hand, and he came up, 'Hello, by George the colony is in a blaze; they have been fighting for the last three months, and they were at it every day.'

WAR! thinks I, the perils, although perhaps not exactly the pride, pomp, and circumstance of glorious war. I heard a voice exclaiming from some corner of the cabin, 'How unfortunate – how melancholy the intelligence', as I was seated beside the captain, and about to unfold a journal called the *Southern Cross*, and I answered, 'Not at all – the best news we could have; present inconvenience, but future and permanent advantage. 'Tis a quarrel that must have come about sooner or later in the natural course of affairs, for there was a deep under-current running, and since it has come let us have it out, and be done once and for all.'

Some stared at me as if I had been a fire-eater, or such like, but the captain and others agreed with me, and I was quite satisfied that, after all, I was not so far in the wrong. We proceeded to skim the news, now that we were about set to leave Neptune's domain.

We sighted two ships of war, which we knew to be the *Curacoa*, 24, and *Miranda*, 15 [guns]. The latter I remember to have specially visited when she was lying in Leith Docks in 1853, and had come down from England under jury masts.

The *Miranda* was commanded by the late Captain Lyons, son of Admiral Lord Lyons,[20] during the Russian war, and she did a great deal of work in the White Sea. I think she was named the falcon of Sir Charles Napier's fleet. In March last, when visiting Greenwich hospital, in company with a scientific friend, a lieutenant of the Royal Engineers, we met the medical officer who had acted as assistant-surgeon of the *Miranda* during the Russian war. He had been newly promoted, and his friends were condoling with him on having to give up a comfortable billet in Greenwich Hospital, in order to take up that generally coveted promotion.

We on board the *Ganges* also ascertained, what we would have rather not known, that the *Ida Zeigler* had arrived before us, for we saw her lying at anchor as we were making sharp tacks up the channel leading to the Auckland roadstead. The *Tyburnia* had also arrived from London, and the *Annie Wilson*, the former having had to go into quarantine, as small-pox was aboard, and the latter having had nine deaths on board.

Captain Funnell may, therefore, congratulate himself on having brought his ship to land in such a healthy, comfortable state, and so may also our zealous, skilful surgeon, Mr. Welby. The cleanliness of the *Ganges* and her airy 'tween decks have called forth general commendation.

The *Ranjitara*, a steamer of 220 tons, was lying at anchor. The last time I saw this vessel was when she was moored in the Clyde, near Finnieston Ferry,[21] and was about to be brought out here under canvas by Captain Mathieson, who is well known as an experienced mariner.

She was now plying in the intercolonial trade, and I may add that she made the passage, from Waterford in Ireland to the North Cape of New Zealand, in 132 days. One of her passengers, belonging to Glasgow, told me that her decks were often wet, which was to be expected in so small a vessel, and moreover, a steamer, not a sailing ship.

We let go anchor at a little past three o'clock [22], when boats came off from the shore with Custom House authorities, medical inspector, Mr. Lusk the surveyor of the colony, the ship's agents, friends of the passengers, and a Volunteer officer in full uniform. We had anticipated the latter functionary, as in the course of the forenoon little Benson, a spirited little Yorkshireman, borrowed an artillery Volunteer coat from Mr. Garrett, a respectable butcher from Greenwich, and attaching a few ribbons to his cap, marched from the forecastle to the stern, playing up 'British Grenadiers' on his bugle. Loud and hearty cheers greeted him in his progress.

The recruiting officer immediately commenced operations, using the capstan for his writing materials. I am not aware what success he had, but I know that several intend to go to the front when they get ashore.

The boatmen told us that the way in which the *Ganges* was handled, while coming up the channel, had excited general admiration. The saloon was regularly invaded by strangers, and the passengers did not appear at all comfortable at seeing others encroach on what had so long been their exclusive domain.

I put on a hat, and felt anything but easy under this rig, then over the ship's side, accompanied by my daughter, and into a boat to be rowed ashore. As it was blowing stiffly we shipped some water and got rather wet, but we were too well seasoned to pay much attention to that incident.

On reaching the quay we proceeded up an extended wooden jetty to the shore. So long as I walked on the smooth wood I did not feel so much out of sorts, for the last land I touched was at the entrance of the Highbury Railway Station, in north London, and since then it has been nothing with me and my children but walking the plank.

We then halted at Stepney, crossed a platform, and were shipped on to another line of rails leading to Tilbury. On reaching the latter point we disembarked on to a platform which led down to a quay – no touching of land, as if Neptune was resolved to make sure of his prey. I there recognised the *Ganges* out in the stream, hailed a boat, and we were soon afloat in our ocean home.

Today I again touched land at the commencement of the quay, and, as Tom Sutton would have said, 'It was deuced uncomfortable', especially when I encountered stones. In truth, I would rather have gone on the tread-mill, than have been compelled to walk as one ought to do along Glasgow's Sauchiehall Street.[23] There was a constant tendency to swing to and fro, and an impatience for the ground to give a bit of a heave, if only to help us on our way. That sensation will have disappeared in a day or two.

When Fox[24] visited Paris at the short peace of Amiens, during the Consulate of Napoleon, he complained that everything wore a warlike aspect. He was a man of peace, although he was wounded in a duel. By way of explaining why he was wounded and not killed, the great statesman jocularly said that his opponent must have used battle powder, there being then an outcry against the quality of the ammunition served out to our troops.

Well, such is the aspect of Auckland at the present time. Most of the regulars, or very much the whole of them, are at the front, but there are volunteers, a naval brigade – the latter not exclusively formed of seamen and volunteer artillery – as well as mounted rifles, cavalry, and militia. In fact, almost every man was armed, or wore some military or naval trappings on his person.

When I marched a little way up from the quay, I met several Maoris, and generally in wretched attire – a piece of blanket, or any cast-away rag of clothing being braced around their persons, and all bare below the knees. They were poor looking creatures, but I came across some who were tattooed, and they were a better-built class and not so repulsive.

One tattooed fellow I saw drinking at a pump, who was in decent European attire, and he looked a strong, well-formed man, who, barring his face, might have passed for a house carpenter or honest artificer with you. These are called friendly Maoris, but they are still looked sharply after, and bands of armed Volunteers are patrolling in every quarter of the town during the night.

I also saw several female Maoris, and I cannot say that they were very attractive, or specimens of feminine loveliness. In truth, they look even worse than the men, though I am told that some of the half-caste women are really comely.

We rejoined the ship a little after six o'clock, and were so pleased to find ourselves once more afloat, and seated down to tea, with a few exceptions who remained on shore.

13 October, Tuesday – I awoke at five this morning, on hearing the boom of the morning gun of Her Majesty's ship *Caracoa* come through my open port – a cheerful sound, thought I, under present circumstances, as it denotes the might that floats under the flag of England.

A little before breakfast, I saw Her Majesty's ship *Miranda* get up her steam, and steer away to the southward, evidently bent on no peaceful mission. However, as yet, I know little or nothing about the details of the war, or the localities of this quarter of the world.

Between five and six a.m. I was out on deck, when a boat came alongside with fresh meat and vegetables, and also brought the news that young Crawford had expired at four o'clock this morning, an event which took none of us by surprise.

I had a talk with the Custom House officer who was placed aboard on our arrival yesterday. He was a knowledgeable man, and once commanded a coaster in New Zealand. Last night he deftly made up a bed for himself on the top of the saloon table, and I threw my sea-coat over his feet, telling him to mind his toes, which was a common expression with us on board.

After breakfast I went ashore, and had a stroll through the place, which I liked very much. It was rather tiring to go very far about, as the pathways were not of the best, and the ascents many and rather steep.

During my rambles I met a butcher from the fishing village of Newhaven, near Edinburgh, with whom I used to formerly deal. He was very much surprised, and not a little gratified, to see me. He told me that he had been out here for five years

– had married since he came – had a place four miles out of town, and was doing very well.

I went down to the quay in the afternoon – for we were also to remain on board this evening, and there I found the captain's barge, in which sat Le Maire and three Jacks, one of the latter being over-jolly.

As the captain was expected at any moment, I coaxed him to take his seat, adjusted the rollocks for him, and put his blade into his hands. When the captain did arrive, with two of the lady passengers, and had laid hold of the tiller cords, off we went. Poor Jack in his first stroke scarcely touched the water, and very nearly went to leeward himself. The sharp eye of the captain soon saw the state of affairs, but he said nothing, as a little licence was now almost inevitable.

In the second stroke Jack plunged his oar deep into the water, and could scarcely fetch it up. But at the third stroke he succeeded better, and really pulled wonderfully well throughout, all things considered. I was glad once more to be on board, for the *Ganges* has been a comfortable home to me.

While I was sitting in our boat before starting, a Maori was engaged in trimming the sails of his fishing boat, which was lying close to us. He wore a cast-off corporal's greatcoat, for I saw the yellow stripes on the arm; and no other article of apparel was visible, though it was charitable to infer that he was encased in some underclothing. From out beneath the coat was seen his long, thick, bare legs.

I gave him a shake by the hand across the gunwale, which I thought was only common civility, seeing I had come so far to see his country. He grinned and was gracious, but he could not be of the better caste, for he was not tattooed.

Our party was small on this, the last evening that we were to spend on board; but we got on very pleasantly, for there has been nothing but harmony among us all in the cabin for the last sixteen weeks.

I learned that 220 blue jackets[25] were ordered to the front today.

14 October, Wednesday – This was a fine day, and the main deck presented a scene of bustle as the sailors, under the direction of Mr. Woolley, were engaged in hoisting the luggage and packages out of the hold, which articles then have to be cleared by the Custom House officer before they go over the ship's side into the lighter.

Old Jacob, the Dane, who was a most ready, good-tempered, and handy sailor, was a sort of privileged person. He had been a little jolly last night, and was consequently a little out of joint today. With the sanction of the purser, I took him into the cabin of Sails to administer to him some medical comfort in the shape of two glasses of port, and Jacob declared that the doctor could not have treated him more skilfully.

Subsequently, I saw Jacob going about the deck arrayed in a hat minus the crown, and profusely decorated with the feathers of some of the sea birds which had been caught. Poor, honest fellow! he looked so jocose as he went about his work.

For the first time I descended into the forecastle among our tars. They insisted that I should take a share of their dinner, which consisted of excellent soup and fresh, stewed meat. They dispensed it with three-pronged forks.

The captain insisted upon us all staying to dinner, which we did, and then down the gangway into the lighter, which had a main and foresail. There was a stiff breeze blowing, but as soon as we got out of the lee of the *Ganges* the lighter came finely up to the wind, and we were at the quay in a trice.

With some difficulty we at length got quarters in the Naval Hotel, kept by Captain Pearson, who has been in almost every ocean, from the White Sea to the Southern Pacific. It is situated on the Karangahapa Road. Our parlour in every corner showed signs that we were in the abode of a seaman – sextants, quadrants, chronometers, charts, representations of ships, and the figureheads of their commanders, with a few six-pounder shot placed on the top of the piano by way of decoration.

The situation and the surrounding scene reminded one of the back part of Dunoon.[26] The resemblance was further heightened by the recollection of a description of the interior of the comfortable habitation of a sea captain from that town, with whom a relative of mine resided one season.

I ought to have mentioned that one of the first items of news that we received from the pilot on Monday was that the mail for Australia and England had departed on the 6th current, and our next opportunity would be on the 1st approximately, of the following month.

1. The Campsies are a range of hills that are the remnants of a long-dormant volcanic outcrop, a few miles to the north of Glasgow.

2. Captain James Cook, 1728–79, navigator sent by the British government, starting in 1768, to explore and chart areas of the globe, but particularly the south seas, New Zealand, which he claimed for Great Britain, and Australia. He made three voyages, and on his last he was killed by rebellious natives in what is now Hawaii, in 1779.

3. The River Tay enters the North Sea (German Ocean) to the east of the city of Dundee, and adjacent to a stretch of sand known as the Drumly sands.

4. Ben Lomond is the highest mountain in the area around Loch Lomond in central Scotland.

5. The River Doon near Ayr in Ayrshire. The Brig o' Doon is much associated with Burns's work 'Tam o' Shanter'.

6. A popular gentlemen's clothing outfitters that traded in central Glasgow for over 150 years.

7. Sir John Franklin, 1786–1847, English explorer who joined the navy at the age of 14 and fought at the Battle of Trafalgar in 1805. He explored Canada and the Canadian Arctic between 1819 and 1827. He was Governor of Tasmania from 1834 to 1845, and then was invited to lead an expedition to the Arctic to find the much sought after North West Passage, said to provide a faster shipping link over the inlets of the north of Canada with the Pacific Ocean. In 1847 Franklin perished during that expedition, and for years afterwards attempts were made to find him and his men and ships the *Erebus* and the *Terror*.

8. A reference to Buchanan's relative's burial being near to that of his wife's grave.

9. Thomas Babington Macaulay (1st Baron of Rothley), 1800–59, born at Rothley Temple in Leicestershire, and educated at Trinity College, Cambridge. He carved out legal, writing and political careers. He was MP for Calne in 1830, and then legal advisor for the Supreme Council of India, 1834–38. He then became MP for Edinburgh in 1839. His work *History of England from the Accession of James II*, published in five volumes in 1848, turned out to be what today would be considered a bestseller.

10. Warren Hastings, 1732–1818, an English-born colonial administrator. From 1750 until 1784 he worked in India with the East India Company. Through the efforts of many of his enemies he was charged with cruelty and corruption, but after a trial that took seven years and 145 sittings, he was acquitted in 1795.

11. Sir Edward George Earle Bulwer Lytton, 1803–73, English novelist, playwright, essayist, poet and politician. As a writer he used the pseudonym of Lytton Bulwer. Although popular during his lifetime, his writings, which include *The Last Days of Pompeii* (1834), are now largely forgotten. He was an MP from 1831 until 1841 for St Ives, and for Herts from 1852 until 1859. He was elevated to the peerage in 1866.

12. Islands in the Hebrides off the Scottish West Highland coast. Iona is of great religious significance, while Staffa contains the much revered Fingal's Cave.

13. Ailsa Craig is a volcanic rock off the Scottish south Ayrshire coast and nowadays a protected bird sanctuary. It was known locally by the nickname of Paddy's Milestone, as one of the last parts of Scotland encountered prior to reaching the Irish coast.

14. The Bass Rock is a large volcanic rock off the Scottish Lothian coast, a few miles south-east of Edinburgh. Also a bird sanctuary at present, it was once the site of a high-security prison.

15. Loch Long and Loch Goil are Argyllshire sea lochs, or what Scandinavians would call fjords.

16. Notorious armed highwaymen and robbers who preyed at night on the many stagecoaches travelling through deserted roads in mainland Britain during the heyday of the mail coach and other stagecoach services.

17. John Wesley, 1703–91, English evangelist and founder of Methodism. He is believed to have travelled 250,000 miles and preached 40,000 sermons during his lifetime.

18. Carmyle was formerly a rural village but is now a suburb in the east of Glasgow, on the north bank of the River Clyde.

19. Royal Exchange Square, in the commercial centre of Glasgow, was a busy banking sector of the city.

20. Admiral Lord Edmund Lyons, 1790–1858, joined the navy in 1803 and served in several campaigns. He was promoted to admiral in 1850, and was Commander-in-Chief of the British Mediterranean fleet 1855–58.

21. The Finnieston ferry was one of several cross-river ferries that operated within the four-mile stretch of harbourage that was known as Glasgow Harbour.

22. An Auckland newspaper the *Daily Southern Cross* noted in the shipping intelligence column in the edition of 13 October 1863, that the *Ganges* from London had arrived in Auckland Harbour on 12 October 1863. In earlier editions of that newspaper dating from 27 August 1863, the vessel had been noted as having been expected for arrival at Auckland.

23. One of Glasgow's main shopping and leisure thoroughfares for over 150 years.

24. Charles James Fox, 1749–1806, English politician born in London, who became an MP at the age of 19. He became a political rival to William Pitt the Younger, and opposed the war with France. When he died in 1806 he was negotiating for peace with France and getting ready to introduce a Bill to abolish the slave trade.

25. Blue jackets were troops recruited from the migrant settlers in New Zealand.

26. Dunoon is the main town and a once busy holiday resort, on the Clyde estuary coast of the Cowal peninsula, Argyllshire.

Auckland

Ashore – And now fairly ashore, and I must this evening spend repose on dry land, much as I may long after my own snug cabin on board the *Ganges*.

I therefore cease to journalise, and am rather in the predicament to which a friend of my father, a writer to her Majesty's Signet,[1] brought the correspondence of an eminent legal firm in Edinburgh, when he was their youngest apprentice, and as such had to keep the letter book.

He was an anxious and industrious, but by no means a bright youth, for instead of affixing a date to the first letter of the particular day, and using an abbreviated phrase for those of that day thereafter, for several successive days he treated the mail with the same phrase, leaving the firm with no means of identifying the respective date for each item of mail. So with me now ashore it will be all anxious scrutiny of my journal, until the departure of the mail for England.

As I have previously written, this place is in a state of very considerable excitement, and most talk is chiefly about the war which is now going on within a few hours ride of it.

I saw the commissariat wagons with their six horses and their three mounted men daily passing under my window with stores to the front, and also the cavalry wending their way to the same destination; and by my troth, it will be no light bill of costs which this war will entail, for I hear that upwards of two millions[2] sterling have been already disbursed. But, it must be carried out, and with spirit.

It would be difficult to exaggerate the determination that animates the colonists. Fortunately there is now a continuous road between this town and the seat of war at Waikato, along which the stores and munitions of war can be readily transported. The wagons leaving this place in the morning halt for the night at Burton's farm, Papakura, and reach their destination in the front by the following afternoon.

Of course, a great number of horses are in requisition, and more were on their way from Australia. This week, ninety-two were landed from Sydney in the fine new steamer, the *Claude Hamilton* (800 tons), which brought the English mails. Only one was lost on the voyage, in consequence of the rough weather and the heavy rolling of the vessel, and that was a mare in foal.

Buchanan made some interesting observations of Auckland as it appeared when he arrived in 1863. This 1865 photograph of part of Queen Street shows a busy combination of photographic, grocery, hairdressing and hotel establishments in one of the main thoroughfares near to the harbour at the time. The colonial feature of the scene contrasts sharply with the various British views illustrated. From the Edward Browse Gilberd Collection, courtesy of the Alexander Turnbull Library, Wellington, New Zealand

I cannot say much for the outward appearance of the vast proportion of the horses. They have a stunted, cadger-like aspect, very like what I have seen in a French diligence. Still, they are hardy animals, and up to their work.

The favourite costume of our colonial horsemen is long boots and spurs: and how they do push over the rough, uneven, ascents and descents of this town. It is rare to see any of them at a trot. A hard gallop and still more rapid pace is the rule. But active measures are being taken to improve the breed.

24 October, Saturday – Today I saw some very fine draught animals and real horses standing in Queen Street. One who has much travelling to do around here would require a horse, for the town or settlement straggles over a great extent of space.

It occurred to me, when I was walking over in the direction of the barracks and Governor's house, and reached a height from which I obtained a tolerably extensive view, that the able city surveyor of Glasgow, would rather go over an area of half a mile of that city, than undertake the survey of Auckland. The value of property in Auckland would of course bear no comparison to that of Glasgow.

As I looked upon the friendly Maoris, that being the term by which they are known here, with the tattoo of their amity upon their arm, I involuntarily thought to myself that it would be about as easy to blend the two elements of fire and water as to hope for any formal or extensive amalgamation between the white and the dark or upper coloured population.

Some of the men are, however, strong limbed fellows. The other day a chief named Metemara came into a bank where my friend Mr. Welby, our surgeon, happened to be present. His height approached to seven feet, and he was most grotesquely tattooed, although otherwise well got up in European costume. He drew £400 in gold, and on leaving the bank made a right stately bow, first to the teller and then to Welby.

Hostile Maoris are known to have been at large, as they have been seen within the precincts of the hospital. They borrow the coat with the badge for the use of their countrymen who are classed among our friends, and then they strut about with perfect impunity, thus making them afraid. It would be rash of me, having only been a few days in the colony, to form any opinion upon the policy pursued, seeing as I was ignorant about the cases which determine it.

But when I learned that these enemies are cruising here under false colours, and purchasing nails and buttons, as also marbles – the latter from the children, and, on the other hand, hear every other day of women, children, and old men having been ruthlessly butchered, and still more savagely, tomahawked in cold blood, I felt roundly inclined to lay by the heels those fellows who are thus endeavouring to recruit their munitions of war.

The great difficulty in this, as in all bush wars – whether with Kaffirs or Maoris – was to bring them to a regular stand up fight. Our foes were too shy to battle – they knew their game too well to be thus caught in the open. We may strafe and harry one of their strongholds, but what do we find? Only the mere husk. The defenders have entirely vanished into the bush. Their strength lies in the bushy, dense nature of the region.

As was said in reference to the Kaffir war,[3] Make law, and that was being done. They were already busily laying the hedging bill, to legalise any weapon that will clear a way through the underwood.

Penetrate and combine is the policy that must always be adopted in any land which contains brave men ready to defend it, and which nature has rendered inaccessible to its people.

Such was the course pursued by the English government in regard to our own gallant Highlanders, when General Wade[4] made those roads, some of which I have passed over, especially that leading over Glencoe, and which opened up the way for the planting of the military inspired towns of Fort William, Fort George, Inversnaid, and others. That was the policy of the illustrious Chatham,[5] who converted what had been a thorn in the side of the Imperial Government into a weapon that has since nobly sustained Britannia in innumerable and brilliant combats in every quarter of the globe. Why, they were among the bravest of troops.

A younger brother of my father, a sailor, steered one of the boats containing Highland soldiers through the surf, as they were proceeding to the battle of the Blue Mountains,[6] when one or two of the other boats were swamped, and those on board perished. The Highland officer was interfering with my kinsman in the conduct of the boat, when he sternly ordered him to, 'shut up', as he and not the officer, was in command, and was responsible for the lives of that officer and all his men. The Highland soldiers were frightened at the rude surge, for they were not in their own element; but as soon as they got through the surf, and laid hold of the firm land, up went their martial spirit at the sound of the pibroch, and they shouted in their homely phrase – 'Come noo, lads, let's get the beggars, go get at them!'

The climate here is delightful, so far as I have yet experienced. We were now at the close of October, but that period was very different with us here from what it is back in Glasgow. There, everyone is preparing to encounter the November chill and fog. We are looking forward to summer, if, indeed, it has not already arrived – for I have never, unless perhaps on some very rare and beautiful day in early September, felt the atmosphere so soft and pleasant as it is in this clime. And yet here, the acclimated colonists have been complaining of the weather during the last few days as having been fickle – raining and blustering at intervals, with sunshine between. Well, when it does rain here it does so in earnest.

Here we are situated on an isthmus, it being only some six or seven miles across to the opposite sea at Manukaw, where H.M.S. *Orpheus* was lost last year. The location exposed Auckland more to the influence of certain winds.

It is in vain, when such rains are descending, and such stout winds blowing, to seek the shelter of that article, which is called an umbrella. The best resource is to don waterproof clothing, and go forth to face it, as I had to do the other day, when due at 12 o'clock at the Q.E.C. Hotel (Quality, Economy, and Civility, though we jokingly read it as, Questionable Characters Entertained.) We went there to attend a meeting of the subscribers to a testimonial to be presented to Captain Thomas Funnell, of the good ship *Ganges*.

We finalised our arrangements, and a deputation of four of us was appointed to proceed on board and inform the captain of our presentation. When we got to the quay we found that the traffic with the shipping in the roadstead was suspended, in consequence of the rainy, boisterous state of the weather. However, we selected a tight-looking boat, named the *Louisa*, and her owner agreed to take us out for double fare.

As the distance was short, there was only a little way to pull before we got under the lee of our ship, and it was accomplished with comparative ease. We returned in one of the fine boats of the *Ganges*, under the charge of our faithful Woolley and four of our sailors.

28 October, Wednesday – Today we have had much rain, with rather thick cloud, which will be trying for our troops at the front. A Lieutenant Spencer Percival was interred yesterday. I heard, through someone who was present at the funeral, that the body of this fine young man, who died so heroically, was frightfully mangled; indeed, I stopped him in the middle of the recital, as the details were so revolting.

29 October, Thursday –. This day was a lovely one, following as it did the heavy rain of yesterday. The leaf is now falling in Glasgow, and nature going to sleep. Here she is reviving, and sending forth her fruits in the shape of early potatoes, cabbages, cauliflower, etc. The flowers are richly tinted and beautiful, especially the lily of the Nile. The palm tree may also be seen growing in all directions.

We have a great variety of fish. There is a species called the Kaura, which tastes very well, being a sort of a cross between the salmon and the mackerel. It is caught in great abundance by the Maoris, who seem to be the only professional fishermen here. There are also herrings, and abundance of mussels and oysters; the latter choice shell-fish can be gathered in bushels by anyone who chooses to repair to nearby Freeman's Bay at ebb tide, and it is within half an hour's walk of where I am now. There is, however, one drawback, and that is that one dare not swim, on account of the sharks which abound along the shores.

We were now in an abnormal condition or state of war, and every one capable of bearing arms had to take his turn of picket duty within the town, while the young men have to go in rotation to the front. Most of the *Ganges* steerage passengers (and they are not liable to military duty for three months after landing) have found a job.

As to the resources of the colony, I know little other than what may be found in several published works. But Glasgow's accomplished chamberlain, Dr. Strang,[7] if he was here could, I have no doubt, soon unravel the statistics of the colony. He once sat alongside the fair Eugenie of France,[8] and described to her the more striking features of Glasgow's vast hive of industry, while the State Barge followed in their wake.

The volunteers who were to form the picket near to me for the night are marching to the guard-house. They have few military trappings beyond their belts, Enfield rifles, and cartouche boxes; but they look like men who would not flinch in their work. A glance at them satisfies me that they are men who have roughed it, and are prepared to rough it again.

As I go down the streets many a salutation do I get from the *Ganges*es, or my fellow passengers, for there is a camaraderie among us. Often, as I have contemplated them standing in groups about the decks on a quiet night, I thought of the various parts of England, Ireland, and Scotland from whence they were gathered.

Since my earliest recollections, I have always had a sympathy with sailors and salt water. I remembered a boy, who belonged to a village on the banks of the Dee, that sweet spot where I was nurtured, and who went to sea. His name was John Turnbull, and he was several years my senior.

John, or Jack as he came to be termed, returned in due course, and for a time was our village hero. I have a dim recollection of him ascending and getting through a sort of port-hole in the roof of the parish church, where my worthy grandad hebdomadally held forth. I think he had been in search of the nests of bats, or of some other and more proper birds.

And how nicely did Jack affix an iron keel to a little toy ship of mine; and how proud was I when I saw it then float so steadily in the slack of the current of that beautiful stream, on the banks of which our gracious Lady the Queen Victoria did select her Highland home.[9]

I had then not seen the sea, and had many fanciful ideas of it – the reigning one being that it would resemble the River Dee multiplied many times; and how gratified I was when, afterwards, I was led down Marischal Street, Aberdeen, to obtain a view of the sea as it stretched far out to the coast of Norway.

During that, my first visit to the Granite City, which rejoiced in the motto *Bon Accord*, I was taken to see our friend Dr. Ogilvy, of Midmar, then an old man in his dotage. In his early days he had mixed with Johnson, Goldsmith, Sir Joshua Reynolds, Garrick, Edmund Burke, and the rest of that galaxy, as you will find described in James Boswell's *Life of Johnson*.

In later days, when I was either a dog or a tiger in Mr. Carson's class in the High School of Edinburgh – *i.e.*, either in the third or the fourth form, certainly before I got among the lions, or the fifth form and the Rector's class, where the still surviving Professor Pillans then ruled – I recollect that my father's neighbour came to be Captain, afterwards Rear-Admiral, Gourly.

He was in a position not uncommon then among naval officers. He had no great friends in the State, and he was too proud to go out of his way to seek them, far less to cringe to the powers that be about his finances. Lord Collingwood,[10] that gallant and good man, to whom he subsequently owed his commandership, wrote on one occasion to the effect – 'As for Lieut. Gourly, I have to state that he fought his boat until it sunk under him.' He was married, had a family, and nothing save his pay to support them.

Lord Cochrane,[11] his exploits, and his maltreatment by the Government, came to mind, when Captain Gourly described an interview that he had with that naval hero, when he was suffering imprisonment on the foul and, as it afterwards proved to be, most false, calumnious charge of having conspired to raise the public stocks, by putting in circulation a fictitious report as to the great Continental war then pending.

When the captain entered the apartment of Cochrane, the latter shook his brother seaman warmly by the hand, saying, 'Gourly, I wonder that you are not afraid to call and be seen with me. Why, my good fellow, it will stop your promotion.' To which the captain answered, 'No, no; never think of that; I yet expect to see your Lordship, First Lord of the Admiralty, and then perhaps you will do something for my poor boy.'

Lord Cochrane then rummaged for some papers, which he showed to the captain as proofs of his innocence. Gourly recoiled from their touch as if he was stung at the very idea that he could ever doubt the honour of his fellow-warrior.

That poor boy bore his father's untarnished name, John Gourly, and followed his own honourable profession, being a gallant lieutenant in the Royal Navy. One Monday that fine young man walked to Lochend, near Edinburgh, to view the skaters. Shortly after his arrival, crash went the ice beneath a young gentleman skater.

Young Gourly paused not an instant, but instinctively flew to the rescue. Both perished. I shall never forget that Monday evening, when the cart containing the corpse arrived, and one of the daughters lay on a sofa in my father's house, enveloped in a blanket. That girl was afterwards married to M. Emile de Bonne Chose, a literary man in Paris, whom I subsequently met with his lady in Edinburgh.

Honourable mention was made of him by Sir Walter Scott in one of his letters from the French capital (see Lockhart's Memoirs of Sir Walter). Another, and the elder, daughter perished off the Isle of Wight, the ship in which she had made the voyage from the island of Nevis, West Indies, having been wrecked there near – too near – to the land.

There arose a cherished and lasting friendship between our two families. A brother and also a daughter of my own, both now deceased, bore the name of that fine old seaman and most truly sincere and humble Christian, who died at peace with all men, 11 years ago, aged 85, after having been 74 years listed on the books of the Admiralty.

A few years previous to the death of Admiral Gourly it was my lot to converse with the gallant Cochrane, then Earl of Dundonald, about Admiral Gourly, whose last service afloat had been to convey the effects of Lord Collingwood, on the death of the latter while Commander-in-Chief of the Mediterranean fleet, to his sorrowful, grieving widow, Lady Collingwood, in England.

Little did I ever expect to know Lord Dundonald, for whom from boyhood I entertained a hero-worship. One can read of his many brilliant achievements, with such actions as – the *Speedy* (54 guns and some 4 pounders) taking the Spanish *Sebeque*, with upwards of 300 men, and more than 50 guns of very different calibre from those on board the daring little *Speedy*.

Then there was the affair at Basque Roads,[12] where, as the Emperor Napoleon said at St. Helena, if Cochrane, in the *Imperieuse* (50), had been seconded as he ought to have been by the fleet outside under Lord Gambier,[13] not a French ship could have escaped destruction.

In one of my last letters to Lord Dundonald, in January, 1859, I happened to refer to that expression of opinion by Napoleon, when I received a letter from Mr. Erpe, his Lordship's secretary, followed by another from himself, saying they were aware Napoleon had so expressed himself, but desiring to know my authority for that statement. I referred them to the work of Baron Lee Cases,[14] *Conversations with Napoleon at St. Helena* being the title, if I remember correctly.

But I fear that I begin to prattle out of fashion, and I hear the tramp of armed men at this moment, 9.51 p.m., beneath my lattice, and the sound of the officer's sword.

And that reminded me that I was writing about Lord Dundonald and of whom it had been most truly written, that Dundonald had all the daring of Nelson, and was his superior in nautical science. His country never threw the gates of glory fully open to his genius and heroism; but he forced open this said glory's gates in another hemisphere, and under another than the dear old union flag that has so often braved the battle and the breeze.

He cut out the defences from under the guns of Callao.[15] (See, *Voyage of Captain Basil Hall*,[16] in H.M.S. *Conway* (24), on the west coast of South America.) The *Conway* was afterwards in the first Chinese war, about 1840–41,[17] under the command of Captain Bethune (of the Cardinal Beaton family,[18] the name being identical). She was subsequently the guard ship, or that of the Admiral, on the Queenstown or Cork station. She was latterly, and may be still, the school [training] ship at Liverpool.

He influenced the destinies of Chile, Peru, and Brazil – for his foes came to tremble at the name of Cochrane, which was a tower of strength. At our last interview, which occurred in the summer of 1854, during the Russian war,[19] he called upon me, and our conversation naturally turned upon the events then passing.

He expressed his opinion to me, roughly and roundly, in the language indigenous to British seamen, as old Lord Hermand had said, and to the effect that, 'we had got into a most damnable hobble'. He also said – for I well recollect the words of that remarkable man – that if he had got the command of the Baltic fleet he would have attacked.

Then he told me that he had been attending the Scottish Peers' election that forenoon, and that he had worn his decorations conferred by various Powers, and which for the last 24 or 25 years he had the permission of his Sovereign to wear. On that expression he suddenly unfastened his closely-braced surtout and bared his breast to me, covered with medals, stars, and crosses, all glittering in their effulgence. My eyes were dazzled with the display.

May all our sailors upon all our oceans follow in the wake, and be guided by the light, of that illustrious but ill-used man. May Britannia say to them, what, alas! she failed to say to him – You will never be forgotten!

---

1. A solicitor within the Scottish legal system.

2. About £197 million at current values. See note 6 for June, 1863.

3. Conflict between British and Boer settlers in South Africa.

4. General Wade, after the abortive Jacobite rising of 1715, was ordered by the British government during the period 1720–40 to survey and open up much of the virtually impassable areas of the Highlands of Scotland with a series of interconnected roads.

5. William Pitt, 1st Earl of Chatham (Pitt the Elder), 1706–78. Politician, statesman and orator, he was educated at Eton and Trinity College, Oxford. He entered Parliament in 1735 and was a Secretary of State in 1756. When leader in Parliament he vigorously pursued the war against France. He was said to have had a magnificent voice which enhanced his oratorical abilities. His final speech to Parliament in 1778 forced a victory over attempts to sue for peace on any terms with the American colonists, which eventually led to the War of Independence.

6. A search of the records has failed to unearth details of this battle. It is possible that Buchanan may have been thinking of some other battle. Given his description, it is possible that he may have been referring to the Battle of Blueberg on 8 January 1806, during the wars with France. In 1796 Britain had occupied the Cape Colony. It was returned to Dutch control in 1803, but the resumption of the Napoleonic Wars saw it being reoccupied in 1805 with conflict erupting shortly thereafter. A British force of 6,600 men, including Highlanders, under the command of General David Baird, carried out an amphibious landing at Saldanha Bay in the Cape Colony. They were attacked by a combined French and Dutch force which they defeated, and Baird and his troops then marched south to take and occupy Cape Town. In 1814 the colony was ceded to Britain.

7. Dr John Strang, 1795–1863, was Glasgow's City Chamberlain until his death in 1863. He was the city's official keeper of statistics, and was renowned for his ability to rattle out facts and figures relating to almost any aspect of Glasgow's general, social, commercial and industrial past and present as of that time. He was a great traveller and an accomplished writer away from his civic duties. His most celebrated work was *Glasgow and its Clubs*, which had several reprints over the years.

8. Empress Eugenie, 1826–1920, a Spanish-born noblewoman of exceptional beauty who was consort to Napoleon III of France from 1853 until 1871, when he was deposed during the Franco-Prussian War. After fleeing to England she was befriended by Queen Victoria.

9. Balmoral Castle.

10. Lord Cuthbert Collingwood, 1748–1810, English naval commander who was born in Newcastle upon Tyne. From 1778 his naval career was closely connected with Horatio, Lord Nelson, including a prominent part in the Battle of Trafalgar in 1805, when he was second in command. He was buried beside Nelson in St Paul's Cathedral, London.

11. Thomas Cochrane, 10th Earl of Dundonald, 1775–1860, a Scottish naval commander who was considered one of Britain's best seamen and an equal of Horatio Nelson. He had several spells in Parliament and lobbied against naval corruption. He was convicted of fraud in 1814 but successfully fought to clear his name through the courts. He commanded Chile's navy from 1818 to 1822, and was restored to the British navy as a rear admiral. In 1854 he was appointed rear admiral of the United Kingdom. On the death of his father in 1831 he succeeded him as the 10th Earl of Dundonald. He was buried at Westminster Abbey in London.

12. Although Buchanan refers to the Basque Roads, it is often named the Aix Roads.

13. James Gambier, 1st Baron Gambier, 1756–1833, English naval commander, born in the Bahamas, who was promoted rear admiral in 1795, and was Lord Commissioner of the Admiralty, 1795–1801 and 1804–06. He served as governor of Newfoundland in 1802–04. He fought as commander of the British fleet at the

bombardment of Copenhagen in 1807, and the Battle of Aix Roads in 1809, when he disregarded signals from Thomas Cochrane, but was eventually acquitted at a court martial.

14. Emmanuel Auguste Dieudonné, Comte de Las Cases (1766–1842), French writer and historian who served Napoleon during the Hundred Days and accompanied him into exile on St Helena.

15. Callao is a port a few miles to the north of Lima in Peru.

16. Basil Hall, 1788–1844, born at Dunglass, East Lothian, Scotland and educated at Edinburgh High School. He joined the navy in 1802 and served on the *Leander* (50 guns), in North America. In 1808 he was promoted to lieutenant on the *Invincible*. By 1814 he was promoted to commander and later was stationed in Chinese waters on the frigate *Alceste*. He wrote *Account of a Voyage of Discovery to the West Coast of Korea and the Great Loo-Choo Islands* in 1818. He retired from the sea in 1823 and concentrated on his literary career, having been elected a fellow of the Royal Society in 1816. In 1829 he published a 3-volume work, *Fragments of Voyages and Travels*, based on his many travels.

17. The First Chinese War was in fact what is often called the First Opium War, 1839–42. It began through disagreements between Chinese officials and British merchants trading at Canton over the importation of opium into China, which led to Chinese action against British and Europeans in November 1839. A series of victorious British campaigns resulted in the Treaty of Nanking in 1842, when Hong Kong was ceded to Britain, several ports opened to British trade, and the Chinese had to pay an indemnity of $20 million to Britain.

18. In the late Middle Ages, James Beaton or Bethune, 1470–1539, and his nephew, David Beaton or Bethune, 1494–1546, were Scottish statesmen and Roman Catholic prelates. They strongly supported France and had close connections with the Scottish monarchy. They vehemently supported the persecution of Protestants in both France and Scotland.

19. More commonly known today as the Crimean War.

Appendix 1

Ships' masts and rigging

Before steam- and eventually diesel-powered shipping were developed, sail power was the engine that ploughed ships through the world's oceans. Captain and crew had to understand what kind of rig of sails would serve them best depending upon the speed and direction of the wind. Sails had to be used to the best advantage to take the benefit of what fuel nature provided with the wind that was blowing, or not, at any time during a short or long haul sea voyage.

The *Ganges* was a three-masted vessel, although Buchanan never refers to the type of ship the *Ganges* was other than a brief reference to its being a frigate. It is therefore reasonable to class the vessel purely as a sailing ship for the purposes of explaining the layout and use of the sails.

The masts were the forward or foremast, the mainmast to the centre of the vessel, and the mizzen mast towards the after end or stern. They were constructed in three parts; the lower mast, the top mast and the topgallant mast. The sails were fitted from the yard-arms on each section of each mast. The crew who worked with the sails did so walking on the ratlines, as they were known, which were fitted below the yard-arms.

In the journal, Buchanan regularly described which sails were used, depending upon the prevailing weather conditions. When fully rigged (all sails set) the square sails dominated. They were the primary sails and caught the greatest volume of wind to push the ship forward. From the deck upwards, the foremast contained the fore sail, the fore topsail, the fore topgallant sail and the fore topgallant royal. From the mainmast were unfurled the mainsail, the main topsail, the main topgallant sail and the main topgallant royal. The mizzen mast had the mizzen sail, the mizzen topsail, the mizzen topgallant sail, and the mizzen topgallant royal.

In a light wind, these square sails were supplemented by studding sails which could be carried on the port or starboard (or both) sides of some or all of the square-rigged sails: for example, the fore studding sail, the fore topmast studding sail, and the fore topgallant studding sail; the main topmast studding sail, and the main topgallant studding sail.

The square sails were also complemented by other sails such as the staysails. The staysails were carried between the masts and were named after the mast from which they were hoisted, namely, the fore topmast staysail, the fore staysail, the main staysail, the main topmast staysail, the main top-gallant staysail, the mizzen staysail, the mizzen topmast staysail, and the mizzen top-gallant staysail.

From an angle at the bow of the ship protruded the bowsprit which was a mast from which a form of staysail called a jib was fitted. It was attached between the bowsprit and the foremast and there were two of these, the jib and the flying jib. The staysails and jibs helped to increase the ship's manoeuvrability.

The spanker or driver was a sail fitted from the mizzen mast, and two could be fitted if required called the upper and lower spanker. The upper part was held by a pole called a gaff and controlled by two ropes. It was sometimes known as a gaff-rigged sail, and its purpose was to reduce the angle at which the ship was leaning caused by the wind force upon the sails.

These non-square sails were sometimes referred to as the fore and aft sails which could be altered from one side of the ship to the other for the purpose of altering the ship's course. When the ship's stern crossed the wind it was known as jibbing, and when the bow crossed the wind it was called tacking. Tacking repeatedly from port to starboard and vice versa (sometimes known as beating) allowed the ship to follow a course into the wind.

Appendix 2

Nautical glossary

Aft: An abbreviation of abaft or after, meaning the rear part of the ship or towards the stern.

After companion: The framing and sash-lights on the quarter deck through which light passes to the cabin and decks below.

Barque: A small square-sterned, three-masted vessel with no square sails on the mizzen mast.

Barracouta (or barracuda): A long slender fish usually found in southern oceans.

Billows: A surge of the sea or waves raised by the wind.

Binnacle: A wooden case or box which contains the ship's compass.

Bonita (or bonito): A striped tuna fish found in warm seas.

Boom: A long spar run out from different places in the ship, to extend or boom out the foot of a particular sail, e.g., jib-boom, spanker-boom, main boom, etc.

Bower anchor: Anchors at the bow of the vessel, located on the port and starboard sides. The anchor on the port side is known the small bower and that on the starboard side is called the best bower.

Braces: The braces are ropes that belong to all the yards of a ship, two to each yard; the yards being cylindrical timbers attached to the masts upon which to spread a sail.

Brig: A two-masted square-rigged vessel.

Burster: A sudden burst or force of wind.

Canvas: Cloth made of hemp and used for the sails of ships. When a ship was in motion by means of the sails it was said to be under canvas.

Chops: The entrance to a channel such as the English Channel.

Close hauled: The arrangement of a ship's sails in an effort to sail as closely as possible in the opposite direction to the wind.

Closely reefed: The last reefs (portions of a sail) of the topsails being taken in.

Cross-jack: The lower yard on the mizzen mast upon which a sail called a cross-jack can be set.

Crossing the Line: A nautical term for the crossing the equator, when an age-old ceremony is often held for those passengers and crew crossing the equator by ship for the first time.

Cuddy: A cabin in the after end of the ship below the poop deck for the use of the ship's captain and his cabin passengers.

Dead-lights: Strong wooden shutters made exactly to fit the cabin windows externally, which were fitted on the approach of bad weather.

Dead reckoning: Calculation of a ship's position without the observation of the sun, moon and stars. A position can be discovered by noting the distance sailed as determined by the ship's log, the courses steered by the ship's compass, and rectifying that data by making allowances for currents, etc. The reckoning by that method has to be corrected when an observation of the sun, moon and stars is possible.

Duck: A lighter material than canvas and used for smaller sails.

Easting: The course made good, or gained, towards the east.

Eastward: Sailing to or looking towards an easterly direction.

Fathoming (or sounding): The use of a lead weighted line with measurements, to ascertain the depth of water through which a ship is sailing.

Fetched: To have reached or arrived at.

Fore: The forward, or afore, part of the vessel, looking towards the bow.

Forecastle: The forward part of a merchant ship, under the main deck, where the seamen live on a platform.

Forehold: The part of the ship's hold before the fore hatchway.

Halyards: Ropes or tackles employed to raise or lower sails upon the yards.

Heaving the lead: To haul in the lead line used to ascertain the depth of water in which the ship is sailing.

Jack-a-Tar (or Jack Tar, or Jack, or Tar): A familiar term for a sailor.

Jib: A large triangular sail which extends from the outer end of the jib-boom towards the head of the fore topmast.

Jury mast: A temporary mast which was erected to replace an original which would have been carried away in a gale, etc.

Kelson (or keelson): A line of timber fastening a ship's floor timbers to its keel.

Knot: A unit of a ship's speed, equivalent to one nautical mile per hour.

Latitude: In nautical terms it is the position of a ship to the north or south of the equator.

Lee: The side opposite to that from which the wind is blowing. For example, if the wind is blowing on the port side of the vessel, then the starboard side is the lee side.

Log: A journal into which the ship's daily data is transcribed, as well as any relevant event or happening that involves crew and passengers.

Longitude: In nautical terms it is the position of a ship to the east or west of the meridian line, which denotes the position of zero degrees longitude.

Main deck: The deck which runs for the entire length of the ship.

Man of war: A naval warship.

Mares' tails: A type of cirrus cloud which mariners in the past claimed was the precursor of a good wind.

Marlin lashings: A small line composed of two strands very little twisted and used to fasten any moveable body in a ship, or even about the mast, sails or rigging.

Midships: The middle part of the vessel, either by the length or the breadth.

North-easter: A north-east wind.

Northing: In navigation, the distance made good towards the north.

Northward: Sailing, or looking towards, a northerly direction.

Offing: To keep seaward, well off the land, while under sail.

Old tons register: Ships' cargo tonnage was formerly weighed differently from the commercial method of 20 cwt to the ton. Shipwise, the weight of one ton was calculated as being the equivalent of 42 cubic feet of articles to the ton.

Poop Deck: A deck that was raised over the after part of a spar deck.

Port: Looking forward to the bow of the ship, the port side is the side to the left.

Pull: The act of rowing with oars.

Put about: Go on to the other or opposite tack.

Quarter deck: The part of the upper deck which is aft of the mainmast.

Running rigging: Those ropes and chains which are employed to raise and lower and arrange the sails, and which are in constant use.

Scuppers: Round apertures cut through the sides of the ship at regular distances and lined with metal which allow water to flow off the deck and into the sea.

Signal halyards: Ropes used to haul up sails, flags, etc., to attract the attention of another ship or ships.

Skids: Massive fenders which comprised long pieces of timber formed to match the curve of a ship's side; and to protect it when heavy items were hoisted on or lowered against it.

Smack: A small, single-masted and broad vessel. Used for mercantile or passenger carrying work, they were often distinctive to the place from which they operated: for example, the larger Leith smacks which could reach a size of 200 tons, or smaller types such as the Berwick smacks.

Sounding: See fathoming, above.

Southing: In navigation, the distance made good towards the south.

Southward: Sailing, or looking towards, a southerly direction.

South-wester: A south-west wind, but often it is a slang expression for a useful waterproof hat used by sailors when they encounter bad weather.

Spare spars: A reserve supply of mast pieces, yards, booms, gaffs, etc., for repair or replacement purposes when the ship was at sea, and collected and secured together in a designated part of the ship.

Squall: A sudden gust of wind. A black squall is one with a dark cloud and normally accompanied by heavy rain. A white squall occurs in clear weather without any warning, and when it reaches a ship copious rain accompanies it.

Standing rigging: Those ropes and chains which are comparative fixtures, and support the masts, etc.

Stern gallery: A balcony at the stern or after end of the ship which extends from one side to the other.

Stream: The middle or fast-flowing part of a tide or current.

Tack: To go about and change course from one side to the other, from the starboard to the port tack or vice versa, which is known as tacking.

Taffrail: A curved rail on the upper part of a ship's stern.

Temperature Fahrenheit: Up until the late 20th century temperatures were given in the Fahrenheit scale, as they were on a daily basis with the *Ganges* on its voyage to New Zealand. To convert the given temperature into the modern Celsius reading, the following equation should be used:

$$\frac{TF - 28}{2}$$

so that for a temperature of 80 degrees Fahrenheit, 80 minus 28 equals 52, and 52 divided by 2 equals 26, so that the Celsius temperature is calculated as 26 degrees.

Tons burthen: A ship's carrying capacity by tonnage.

Weather port: When a ship under sail presents either of her sides to the wind, it is then called the weather side, hence the term weather port, or the port side of the ship which is then to the windward.

Weather port braces: The use of ropes for the weather port side, for the purposes of tacking, for example.

Westward: Sailing, or looking towards, a westerly direction.

Windward: The weather side of the ship, or that on which the wind blows.

Appendix 3

Register of passengers disembarked from the Ganges *on 12 October 1863* *

1. Andrew Anderson
2. Eliza Anderson
3. George Anderson
4. James Anderson
5. Jane Anderson
6. John Anderson
7. Anthony Appleton
8. John Aubin
9. Christopher Bailey
10. Harriet Bailey
11. John P. Bailey
12. Elizabeth Baxter
13. Frederick Baxter
14. William Baxter
15. William Baxter
16. Charlotte Beaver
17. Charlotte L. Beaver
18. James Beaver
19. James Beaver
20. Sarah Jane Beaver
21. William Benson
22. William Bragg
23. Edwin Brown
24. James C. Brown
25. Jane Brown
26. Maria Brown
27. Agnes Brownlee
28. Agnes Brownlee
29. James Brownlee
30. Marian Brownlee
31. Thomas Brownlee
32. William Brownlee
33. Anabella Buchanan
34. David Buchanan
35. Elizabeth Buchanan
36. Robert Buchanan
37. Sarah Buchanan
38. Amelia Carey
39. Eleanor Carey
40. Richard Carey
41. William Carey
42. Samuel Carter
43. Hugh Chermside
44. Andrew Clark
45. Charles Clayforth
46. Harrison Clocksworth
47. Arthur Colgan
48. James Colgan
49. John Cook
50. Thomas Crankshaw
51. James Crawford
52. James Francis Crawford
53. John George Crawford
54. Atkinson Crockett
55. Atkinson Crockett
56. Jane Crockett
57. Mary Crockett
58. Sarah Crockett

59. Grace Crombie
60. James Crombie
61. Alice Davis
62. E. Louise Davis
63. Emma Davis
64. Ezra Davis
65. Fanny Davis
66. Isabella Davis
67. Job Davis
68. Susan Davis
69. James Deans
70. Jean Deans
71. Richard Deans
72. James Dick
73. John Dick
74. Jacob Dodd
75. George Dunn
76. Richard Eaton
77. Arthur Fellow
78. Ernest Fellow
79. Mary Ann Fellow
80. Thomas Fellow
81. Walter Fellow
82. William Fellow
83. William Fellow
84. John Fergusson
85. James Finnedy
86. Sarah Finnedy
87. Jerald Fitzmaurice
88. Bridget Galway
89. Robert Galway
90. Annie Garrett
91. George Garrett
92. Harry Garrett
93. James Garrett
94. Kate Garrett
95. Sophia Garrett
96. George Georgie
97. Jean Georgie
98. Martha Gordon

99. Isabella Gow
100. Janet Gow
101. Jemima Gow
102. John Gow
103. Julia Gow
104. Margaret Gow
105. Margaret Gow
106. Mary Gow
107. Nathaniel Gow
108. Nathaniel C. Gow
109. James Graham
110. Peter Graham
111. Maria Gray
112. G. H. Green
113. C. Hanson
114. John Hanson
115. John Harding
116. John H. Harris
117. Christopher Heaps
118. Elizabeth Heaps
119. George Heaps
120. Thomas Heaps
121. George Hill
122. James Hill
123. Robert Hill
124. George Hillier
125. Elizabeth Hobson
126. Thomas Hobson
127. Jane Howie
128. Leonora Howie
129. Robert Howie
130. Robert Hudson
131. Robert Hudson
132. Charles Inman
133. Charles Inman
134. Sydney Inman
135. Ellen Jackson
136. Ellen Jackson
137. James Jackson
138. Jane Jackson

139. Samuel Jackson
140. William Jordan
141. William Joyce
142. Fanny Keat
143. Maurice Keefe
144. Eliza Jan Kemp
145. Emily Jan Kemp
146. Robert Kemp
147. Hugh Kirkwood
148. William Kirkwood
149. William Kirkwood
150. Ada Lawson
151. George Lawson
152. Hannah Lawson
153. Hannah Lawson
154. Joseph G. Lawson
155. Ralph Lawson
156. Elizabeth Lempriere
157. Rebecca Leybourne
158. William Leybourne
159. William R. Lindley
160. Henry Lopdell
161. Agnes Lupton
162. Elizabeth Lupton
163. John Lupton
164. John Lupton
165. Margaret Lupton
166. Mary A. Lupton
167. Roger Lupton
168. Thomas Lupton
169. John Maben
170. Margaret Maben
171. Adelaide Marks
172. John Marks
173. Capt. George R. Marshall
174. Robert McEwan
175. John McFarlane
176. Colin McGill
177. Elizabeth McHarg
178. Donald McKerrell

179. Annette McCathie
180. Christina McCathie
181. David H. McCathie
182. Jane McCathie
183. Jane C. McCathie
184. John H. McCathie
185. William McCathie
186. William McCathie
187. Jane McColl
188. Charles McCormick
189. Charles McCormick
190. Samuel McCullock
191. Nicholas McNiven
192. Lawrence McWatt
193. Sarah McWatt
194. David Miller
195. Isabella Miller
196. Isabella Miller
197. James Miller
198. Martha Miller
199. Caroline Mitcham
200. Isaac Mitcham
201. Sarah Mitcham
202. Sarah Mitcham
203. David Muir
204. Helen Muir
205. Margaret Muir
206. Mary Mullan
207. James Murray
208. William Murray
209. William Nalder
210. Matthew Notman
211. Charles Paul
212. Frederick W. Paul
213. William Philip
214. Isabella Pye
215. James Pye
216. James Pye
217. Janet Pye
218. Margaret Pye

219. Mary Pye
220. John Rawson
221. Margaret Russell
222. William Russell
223. Jane Ryan
224. William Ryan
225. Esther Sampson
226. Frederick Sampson
227. John Scott
228. Helen Scouller
229. Lawrence Scouller
230. Mary Scouller
231. Mary Ann Scouller
232. Robert Scouller
233. Robert Scouller
234. Rachael Shoales
235. Isabella Smith
236. James Smith
237. James Smith
238. Margaret Smith
239. Mary Smith
240. Susan Smith
241. W. Smith
242. Alexander Stevenson
243. Alexander Stevenson

244. Janet Stevenson
245. Margaret Stevenson
246. Margaret Stevenson
247. Robert Stevenson
248. Thomas Stevenson
249. Sarah Stokes
250. Montague Stopford
251. Patrick Sugme
252. Thomas Sutton
253. Thomas Taylor
254. Matthew Vaughn
255. Edward Walker
256. Andrew Warnock
257. James Warnock
258. Mary Warnock
259. Patrick Warren
260. Miss E. Watling
261. Alexander White
262. William White
263. Elizabeth Willan
264. Greenwood Willan
265. Jonas Willan
266. Thomas Willan
267. Thomas Winter

* Source: Auckland City Libraries: Auckland Area Passenger Arrivals, 1838–1886; www.aucklandcity.govt.nz.

Note: There is a discrepancy between the figure of 228 passengers travelling on the *Ganges* that David Buchanan noted in his narrative, and that of the above register held within the Auckland archives. There may have been some duplication or error within the official figures, or it could have been the case that Buchanan's figure was based on a best guess or an erroneous tally given by one of the ship's officers.

Appendix 4

The Ganges

The *Ganges* was built and launched in Boston in 1855. The vessel was acquired by the Willis, Gann & Company's line which traded regularly with the Asian and Australasian continents.

The ship weighed 1,200 tons register and was capable of carrying 3,000 tons burthen. It could carry cargo or passengers or both.

The *Ganges* sailed from Start Point near Gravesend on 23 June 1863 and dropped anchor off Auckland on 12 October 1863, a passage of 111 days.

The ship later sailed from Auckland to Calcutta with an unidentified cargo, and then from Calcutta to London with another unidentified cargo.

In late 1864 the *Ganges* sailed from Queenstown in Ireland, and arrived at Auckland again on 14 February 1865 with another shipload of 472 emigrants. Captain Thomas (or Theodore) Funnell was once again in command of the vessel for the voyage.

The *Ganges*, according to the records, did not visit New Zealand waters again, and the fate of the ship and the captain is unknown after that last recorded voyage to Auckland.

The Willis, Gann line did have other ships which regularly sailed into Auckland and other New Zealand ports, one example being a 1,323 ton wooden sailing ship, the *Matoaka*. Quite often Willis, Gann ships sailed into New Zealand waters under charter by another shipping company, the Shaw, Savill line.

That company had been started by two clerks formerly employed by the Willis, Gann line, Robert Shaw and Walter Savill. They resigned from the company after a disagreement and formed their own company in 1858. Despite their disagreement, they maintained good business relations with their former employers, often chartering Willis, Gann vessels when required.

Bibliography

Primary sources

Auckland City Council, Auckland City Libraries, online archives.

1841 Census, Edinburgh, St Cuthbert District: 40 Broughton Street.

1851 Census, Edinburgh, St Cuthbert District: 27 Raeburn Place.

1861 Census, Glasgow, St George's Parish, Milton District: 168 St George's Road.

Glasgow Post Office Directories, 1859–62.

Scottish Old Parish Registers: Montrose Parish (County of Angus), Birth Registers.

Scottish Old Parish Registers: Gavrock Parish (County of Kincardine), Birth and Marriage Registers.

Secondary sources

Aldworth, Paul (ed.), *Lloyd's Maritime Atlas of World Ports and Shipping Places*, 21st edition, London, 2001.

Belich, James, *Making Peoples: A History of the New Zealanders*, Auckland, 1996.

Brown, Lesley (ed.), *The New Shorter Oxford English Dictionary*, 3rd (revised) edition, Oxford, 1993.

Dupuy, R. Ernest and Dupuy, Trevor N. (eds), *The Collins Encyclopedia of Military History: From 3500 BC to the Present*, 4th edition, Glasgow, 1993.

Gibson, Tom, *The Maori Wars*, London, 1974.

Gordon, Major L. L., *British Battles and Medals*, Aldershot, 1962.

Haswell-Smith, Hamish, *The Scottish Islands: A Comprehensive Guide to Every Scottish Island*, 2nd edition, Edinburgh, 2004.

Matthew, K. C. G. and Harrison, B. (eds), *The Oxford Dictionary of National Biography*, Oxford, 2004.

North, John S., *The Waterloo Directory of Scottish Newspapers and Periodicals, 1800– 1900* (2 vols), Waterloo, Ontario, Canada, 1989.

Ordnance Survey Atlas of Great Britain, London, 1982.

Parry, Melanie (ed.), *Chambers Biographical Dictionary*, 6th edition, Edinburgh, 1998.

Reed, A. H., *The Story of New Zealand*, Wellington, New Zealand, 1945.

Sinclair, Keith, *A History of New Zealand*, London, 1980.

Smith, Robin, *The Making of Scotland: A Comprehensive Guide to the Growth of Scotland's Cities, Towns and Villages*, Edinburgh, 2001.

Smyth, Admiral W. H., *The Sailor's Word Book*, London, 2005 edition.

Thomas, David St. John (ed.), *Murray's Handbook for Scotland* (1894), Newton Abbot, 1971 reprint.

The Times Comprehensive Atlas of the World, 10th edition, London, 2000.

A maritime trilogy by Ray Solly!

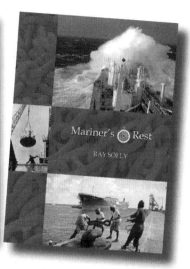

True-to-life adventures of a young man's career which will ring
true with many seafarers – a detailed and enjoyable picture of
the 'Golden Age of Shipping'.

MARINER'S LAUNCH

- *Ray Solly translates his observations into a record of moments of madness, danger, compansionship and hilarity known to all who sent to sea in the post-war period. ...don't miss this book, it really did happen this way.* **Sea Breezes**

ISBN 978-1904445-03-6   £16.95

MARINER'S VOYAGE

A unique narrative of what merchant ship seafaring meant to a young deck officer in the 1960s and 1970s. ...helps capture the whole experience of being at sea. ...A very satisfying account...
The Nautical Magazine

ISBN 978-1904445-50-0   £16.99

MARINER'S REST

- *This is Jonathan Carridia's final years at sea as a senior second and chief officer. He describes in atmospheric terms incidents in the Far East and the initial awe he experienced when joining a very large supertanker.*

ISBN 978-184995-043-5   £16.99

Two tales of two tugboats by Captain Dave Creamer!

RATS, RUST AND TWO OLD LADIES

- *...Creamer tells a good yarn well, such that his book would make an entertaining read for anybody...* **Nautilus UK Telegraph**

- *...a witty, erudite, page-turning read. ...real and armchair sailors may be longing for a similar adventure by the final page.* **International Tug and Salvage**

ISBN 978-1904445-62-3 £18.99

ORIENTAL ENDEAVOUR

- *...His latest work has the same mix of humour and unlikely encounters that has made his sea-going life a rich tapestry of adventure and unforgettable experiences.* **Yachting Life**

- *This is the author's sequel to the highly entertaining, Rats, Rust and Two Old Ladies and an equally enjoyable and well-written tale of two tugboats. ...This is a rollicking tale of the sea, penned with a great deal of warmth and humour, and engagingly entertaining'.* **Nautilus Telegraph**

ISBN 978-184995-034-3 £18.99

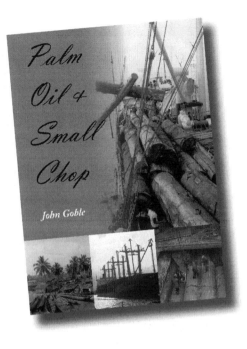

Palm Oil and Small Chop

JOHN GOBLE

'A rare seafarer's memoir ...
and leaping out everywhere
... commentaries loaded with
laughs'. ***Extract from Foreword
by Professor Tony Lane***

- *It is an extremely good read : written in a colloquial, even at times racy, style,
  with some excellent anecdotes and vivid evocations of people and places, I found
  it hard to put down. ...it is a pleasure to follow Goble's precise and informative
  descriptions of such technical aspects of the trade as to how heterogeneous cargoes
  were loaded...* **International Journal of Maritime History**

- *Told sympathetically, yet with a keen eye for the absurd and downright funny,
  this is a lively and colourful story of ordinary people trying to make a living in a
  world where events change their lives irreversibly. I would highly recommend the
  book to our readers.* **Shipping Today and Yesterday**

ISBN 978-184995-011-4   £16.99

That Curious Fellow Captain Basil Hall, RN

JAMES MCCARTHY

Quote from the author –

'*While many naval men in Hall's time made important contributions to the natural sciences, rather fewer made a significant mark in the field of literature. If not unique, Hall was unusual in combining a very active naval career with a prolific authorship of popular works of travel'.*

- *...If ever a man became known for his own curiosity, it was Basil Hall who was able to share his own adventures and travels by becoming a very popular author in his own right. ...a readable, fascinating and probing insight into one of Scotland's most overlooked individuals.* **Ned Middleton**

ISBN 978-184995-033-6   £18.99

To order any of our books, please contact

Whittles Publishing, Dunbeath, Caithness, KW6 6EG
tel: 01593 731-333   fax: 01593 731-400   e: info@whittlespublishing.com

www.whittlespublishing.com